TO DARE
MIGHTY
THINGS

TO DARE MIGHTY THINGS

A Guide to an
Out-of-this-World Life

KEVIN J DEBRUIN

Originally self-published by DeBruin Enterprises, LLC printed in hardcover by Ingram Content Group, 2023.

Self-published simultaneously by DeBruin Enterprises, LLC printed in hardcover by Amazon, 2023.

IBSN Hardback: 979-8-218-08289-5
IBSN Audiobook: 979-8-9876402-0-3
IBSN eBook: 979-8-9876402-1-0
Library of Congress Control Number: 2023901255

Published 2023 in Los Angeles, CA.
Printed in the United States of America.

To Titan:

You're the reason I'm still here

CONTENTS

DARE MIGHTY THINGS

Far better it is **to dare mighty things,** *to win glorious triumphs, even though checkered by failure, than to rank with those timid spirits who neither enjoy much nor suffer much, because they live in the gray twilight that knows neither victory nor defeat.*
–THEODORE ROOSEVELT, APRIL 10, 1899[1]

"Dare Mighty Things" is a saying that is lived by the team at NASA's Jet Propulsion Lab, better known as JPL.[2] You may know the phrase from the famous Teddy Roosevelt quote above, but we were reminded of it by former JPL Director Dr. Charles Elachi when he spoke at a press conference in the final hours of the Mars Curiosity rover flight before its successful landing on Mars on August 5, 2012. He said, "This is a message to the whole world: We are to dare mighty things, even if we might fail. Every explorer has had tough days. It was never easy."

"Dare Mighty Things" lives on the wall in the entrance to Building 180, where the director's office is. It's seen on numerous shirts, cups, mugs, and so on, and is the inspiration for the cover design on this book—I took it from a shirt designed by the JPL store, with JPL's blessing. It's baked into missions via Easter eggs like in Morse code for the Mars Perseverance lander's parachute. "Dare Mighty Things" runs through the blood of all JPLers as they create missions exploring Earth, the solar system, and the universe beyond.

INTRODUCTION

THE FACT THAT you can read this book is proof that what I teach in the following pages *works*.

It works not just to help you level up and achieve your dreams, but also to rescue you from the darkest of times.

The proof comes in two forms. First, the fact that you are reading this book demonstrates that I survived a very, very dark period in 2021. I would not have made it through alive without the mentality and practices I am going to teach you. Second, the fact that I achieved my initial dream of becoming a NASA Rocket Scientist and more recently of being an entrepreneur shows that this mentality can help anyone achieve their dreams.

The lowest point in my life came September 3, 2021. I contemplated suicide. I journaled about it but was afraid even to write down my real feelings. I was scared to write the word. I had the most emotional pain I've ever felt—deep depression and loneliness. I understood why someone would want to take all the pain away.

Now, you might be wondering, "Kevin, why was it so dark?" Here's a quick overview...

My 2021 Knock-Downs:

- In January, after being self-employed for almost two years, I lost all of my income streams.

- In February, I filed for divorce (removing a best friend and a dog from my family), and my ex drained my bank accounts. It was a secret marriage, so I had to tell my family and friends I had been keeping this secret from them for years.
- In March, I had to move to a bad neighborhood and buy all new house things. I was audited and had to pay fines for ignorant past behavior of taxes on the part of myself and my ex.
- In May, I had a two-week depressive breakdown, got in a motorcycle accident, and couldn't exercise for seven weeks.
- In June, I finalized the divorce settlement where my ex-wife went back on every financial agreement we had made previously.
- In July, I received a cease-and-desist regarding a new company I had launched, which cost me a $3,000 investment. I had to borrow money for rent. I didn't get any of the jobs for which I applied or auditioned.
- In August, I made an emergency flight home to Wisconsin to see my deteriorating grandpa and restart my divorce paperwork because the courts had rejected it.
- In September, my grandma died unexpectedly. We had the funeral the day before my birthday. I withdrew from a fitness competition I had trained three months for— the one thing that had been getting me through the past several months. Ten days later my grandpa died, and I had to make a third emergency flight to Wisconsin.
- In October, I had to go from self-employed back to an old engineering job to stave off yet more debt. The court rejected our divorce paperwork yet again. A collection agency came after me for my ex-wife not paying her cable bill.
- In November, I borrowed a hefty sum from my family for rent and bills.
- In December, my dog and best friend Titan landed in the veterinary ICU on Christmas Eve.

The main reason I decided not to hurt myself was I looked at my dog Titan and knew that if I did, then I was also murdering Titan. No one ever came to visit or check on me. It was the pandemic, I lived in Los Angeles while my family and best friends were in Wisconsin, and my California friends were an hour's drive away. So if I died, Titan would eventually die a slow, painful death himself. I could not allow that to happen.

I'm going to go a level deeper here with you all and really show you the darkness of my "Space," my life. The rest of this book will be uplifting, motivating, and give you the confidence you need to take the next step toward achieving your dreams with **NASA's Design Levels** and **The Practices**. But to truly do that, I first need to show you just how low I was. To demonstrate by my own story how you can come from anywhere, overcome anything, and gain trust in yourself, your future, and thrive in any situation.

Here's my journal entry from September 3, 2021:

9/3/2021: "I'm in a really bad head space. I'm anxious, sad, and fearful. I just want someone to be here with me. I don't want to talk to anyone about it. I just need a loved one close. I'm struggling so hard & no one knows or seems to care enough to check in on me. I'm depressed, lonely, have scary thoughts, I understand now why people want to end their pain. I get it. I'm afraid I'll get to a similar place as Robin Williams or Anthony Burdain if I don't make some serious changes. I'm not sure what those changes are."

When I heard people talk about suicide before, I really couldn't relate. I felt bad but couldn't fathom it. Now, I can. I have thought about a lot of questions since that time:

- Why did I not commit suicide?
- How did I not lean into my pain and think only about myself?
- Why did I suffer on and consider Titan?
- How did my mind even go to that train of thought after hitting rock bottom?
- What allowed me to not take my own life and still be here today to tell you about it?

The answer to all of them is the same: I've been doing my best to incorporate NASA Design Levels and a set of habits I call The Practices into my life for the last decade, which gave me a **Phoenix Mentality**, all of which I'll teach you in this book. Without even knowing it, I had been preparing myself to make it through the darkest moment in life. I knew that these habits would help my overall life to achieve goals and help me ride through the rough times, but THIS rough? I couldn't fathom I'd ever get to the place I was on September 3.

I am so grateful that I really started putting conscious effort into my personal development and growth journey in 2015, expanding upon habits I started incorporating in college. I truly believe that this is the reason that I am here today writing to you. I'm proud that you have picked up this book. Let's get started or further develop your own personal growth.

I'll share with you the steps that I used to thrive in both my bright days and my dark days. The process is the same, and it's what NASA uses to design spaceships. No joke, the same thinking can help you accomplish your goals. We will go through all of them in Part 2. I applied these in my life to become a NASA Rocket Scientist and more recently to succeed despite darkness.

Together with the NASA process, I am going to give you tools to thrive through chaos—The Practices. We will go over them in Part 3. These Practices will give you the Phoenix Mentality: a mindset to make it through your journey, whether that's just a delayed launch or a total catastrophe.

I survived 2021 with the aid of my Phoenix Mentality, and more—I also THRIVED in some areas of life.

- Launched a new company in a thirty-day time span
- Ran a 5:30 mile (after recovering from my motorcycle accident)
- Finished first place in the second-toughest Spartan Race
- Celebrated six years sober
- Partnered with a production company for a space TV show
- Improved relationships with my friends and family

I also started this book—and I did so at my lowest point, in September 2021. I needed to find meaning for my suffering. I told myself, "My suffering means that someone else doesn't have to experience theirs—or that I can provide them with the tools, the hope, to not only make it through but also to be able to thrive in the chaos."

That's why I wrote this book: To help you thrive in chaos, no matter how bad it is, and also to help you level up, no matter where you are. What I will teach you will help you no matter what.

Okay, cool, Kevin—but why are you qualified to write this book? They (who are "they," anyway? Aliens?) say I've accomplished a lot in my life. I'm an Eagle Scout; was the captain and MVP of my high school soccer team and went to the state playoffs; have degrees in mechanical engineering and an advanced one in aerospace engineering, as well as a minor in business administration; worked for NASA designing spaceships (I'm literally a Rocket Scientist and have sent stuff to space); have given TEDx talks, written books, and spoken on stage to audiences of over ten thousand people; have traveled the country; taught space camps in South Korea and across the United States; have been on TV; have been a resident Rocket Scientist for media companies; hosted a 13M+ subscriber YouTube channel; have been a competitive bodybuilder, certified personal trainer, and American Ninja Warrior; am an engineering consultant; and am an entrepreneur who launches and runs his own companies.

Okay, enough bragging. The point is, I have accomplished a lot using these tools.

Yet none of that sparked this book. My life went supernova (you know, exploded spectacularly), and it's only because I was living my life with the tools and habits in this book that I didn't fully collapse in on myself and turn into a black hole, never to escape.

No matter who you are or where you're at in life, the methods and tools in this book will remove your launch locks and send you to the stars. And, as an added benefit, they'll also help you if your mission goes awry. When things get bad, The Practices and the Phoenix Mentality can help you rescue yourself, as I learned all too well in 2021. There may come a time when you experience something truly dark in yourself. I hope you never do, but know that you can make it out. I'm here to tell you it's possible. Start preparing now for the unknowns in your future. Whatever the rough road will be, you'll be able to ride it out. It won't be easy, it won't be enjoyable, but you will survive, and this book will give you tools to be ready.

I knew I had to share this with the world, with you.

I had the dream of working for NASA but didn't know how to make it a reality. I wish I had had this book ten years ago—it would have saved me a lot of time and struggle. I had all this excitement, but I was confused, lost, and getting rejected time and time again. My journey into NASA was riddled with hurdles. I sent in 150 applications over three years before I got my first NASA internship. Today I am an experienced NASA Rocket Scientist—exactly what I dreamed I could become. (A hundred and fifty applications! When do *you* quit? After one try? Two? Five?)

Even after that internship, obstacles cropped up. Georgia Tech initially rejected my application to graduate school. NASA's Jet Propulsion Lab, aka JPL, interviewed me but did not give me a job at first. (More on my journey getting into NASA later.)

I get asked all the time why I never gave up, why I kept pressing on despite all the rejections, and I could never really give a good answer. But now, now I have my answer: the NASA Design Levels and The Practices. The NASA Design Levels taught to me by NASA JPL and The Practices I picked up along the way explained to me how I was able to achieve my dream and have accomplishments through my dark ages. This realization was profound to me. All of a sudden, everything made sense. The puzzle pieces came together, my mission was detailed, and the components integrated together.

I am more confident in that answer than anything else because after that realization I started looking at some famous individuals who overcame failure and achieved things people thought were impossible, and I was shocked to learn they employed the same methods and practices I had. I shouldn't have been shocked. I mean, these people achieved feats to the individual similar to that

of the moon landing to NASA. I call them **Famous Launchers.**
We'll look at the patterns of their behaviors in the coming chapters.

I also wish I had had this book once I got my dream job at NASA,
because I sensed something was off. I didn't feel that I was living
up to my full potential. Yeah, I know I was now a NASA Rocket
Scientist, a dream job people would kill for, but I yearned for more.
I wasn't entirely happy and knew that there was more out there for
me. I felt like a trapeze artist without another trapeze bar to grab.
I felt at an impasse. I had just achieved what I wanted, but I didn't
feel fully alive, so I ventured out to discover what would do that. If
I had had this book back then, that discovery would definitely have
been an easier process and I would have felt a lot more confident as
I went through it. I was stumbling around in the dark, finding my
own way. If only I had someone or something to guide me through
it. You're lucky, because you do—me!

In **Part 1—The Proof**, I lay out examples through history of
individuals and technologies that defied limits and disrupted the
status quo to show you that even in the face of worldwide adversity
and stubbornness, one can break through the noise and create
change. These are known as **Disruptors.** Then in **Part 2—The
Process**, I share the NASA Design Levels that were fundamental
for me and several notable figures, aka Famous Launchers, to
overcome obstacles and achieve our dreams even in the lowest
seasons of life. In **Part 3—The Practices**, I give you the main tools
that allowed me and the Famous Launchers to accomplish our
goals. These also granted me my survival of 2021.

Each of The Practices includes several exercises which I **Dare**
you to do throughout the chapter. Take your time with each one,
because these activities are what will create your Phoenix Mentality.
The Phoenix Mentality came from The Practices I've learned
from these incredible individuals, these Famous Launchers, and

incorporated into my life. The phoenix is a mythical bird, not of immortality, but of perpetual mortality. Every time it is struck down, it is reborn from the ashes stronger than before.

That is what I am aiming to create within you. It is inevitable that you will be struck down, and every time you are, those of us who have the Phoenix Mentality will pull ourselves back together, pick up the pieces, and reform ourselves to an improved design. The strike-downs are our life's most intense lessons. They can be anything from a common rejection of "no" when you pitch something to a complete life crisis—things like my experiences during 2021 (you know, the income loss, divorce, motorcycle accident, loneliness, death of both grandparents, all things that devastated me at the time but have forged me into a stronger being).

Combining the NASA Design Levels and The Practices will empower you to achieve an orbit previously unfathomable. Seriously, the combination of these two elements creates the equation $1 + 1 = 3$. (As a Rocket Scientist with seven classes of math past Calculus 1, I can actually prove $1 + 1 = 3$ with mathematical proofs,[3] and no, I'm not joking.[a]) My 2021 experience is an extreme example of this, but I experienced many lows and challenges in my life as I figured out my path into NASA. I'll go into that more in the first chapter. I had some of The Practices in my life at that point, but I wish I had a lot more. We'll also see some of our Famous Launchers overcoming extreme adversity, which is only possible with the Phoenix Mentality.

---

a   Start with the following simple equation: $a = b$
(step 1): Multiply both sides by b: $ab = b^2$
(step 2): Subtract a^2 from both sides and factorize: $ab - a^2 = b^2 - a^2$
(step 3): $a(b - a) = (b + a)(b - a)$
(step 4): Simplify and add 1 to both sides: $a = b + a$
(step 5): $a + 1 = b + a + 1$
Now since $a = b$ (the starting point of this proof), we can write this as: $a + 1 = 2a + 1$
And in the case where $a = 1$, we have: $1 + 1 = 2 + 1$
So, therefore, $1 + 1 = 3$

Finally, in the **Resources** section you will find a list of **Success Support Tools,** which are activities that you can do at any point in your journey.

Come with me on this trajectory as we uncover the secret sauce, the rocket fuel, to launch you into your limitless dreams through a wormhole to otherworldly places or awaken you from a nightmare and pull you out of a black hole. I promise you that the methods and tools in this book will give you the confidence, motivation, and hope you need to get through darkness and send you to the stars. And yes, it will be full of space puns.

Part 1—The Proof

Part 2—The Process

Part 3—The Practices

CHAPTER ONE
My Own Story

*The first principle is that you must not fool yourself
and you are the easiest person to fool.*
–RICHARD P. FEYNMAN

PEOPLE LIKE TO put limits on things they don't understand, on things that scare them, on things they don't believe in. That could be massive technological advancement, winning a sporting event, or even getting a dream job. That last part, that's my story. Below is an abbreviated version, and if it sparks some additional reading interest in you, I detailed my full journey in my memoir *To NASA & Beyond.* Now, let the highlight (and darklight) reel commence.

For just a moment here, let me throw humility out the window and make an unapologetic introduction of why you should listen to what I have to say. I am an expert in NASA's mission and spacecraft design process. I have achieved pretty much every goal I've ever set, and I share my space and success knowledge to educate and inspire others. I craft engaging stories to share my expertise with the world in an easy-to-understand and relatable way. From describing the best place to find alien life in our solar system to overcoming obstacles to achieve your dreams, I try to motivate all those I interact with.

My credentials include:

- NASA Rocket Scientist
- Master of Science in Aerospace Engineering from Georgia Tech
- Designing more than thirty advanced space missions and spacecrafts
- Author of *To NASA & Beyond*
- Two-time TEDx speaker
- Founder of Space Class
- Well-respected and trusted space expert and personality, expert space consultant for media companies
- Spacecraft design course instructor
- Contract engineer for the aerospace industry
- Eagle Scout
- Certified personal trainer
- American Ninja Warrior
- Bodybuilder
- First-place finisher in obstacle-course races

Now let's jump in the deep end. (An aside: Did you know we've explored space more than our own ocean? It's harder to explore the ocean. There is stuff there, water. Space is empty. Easy. Anyway, back to the depths of my ocean life.) My biological father was physically, mentally, and emotionally abusive to me, my brother, my sister, and my mother. My earliest memory is watching him throw my mom against the kitchen cabinets. They eventually divorced, and my mom married the man I call Dad. Thanks, Mike (Dad), for raising me the right way and leading by example to show me what a good person looks like. (More about Dad in chapter 15.)

But wait! There's more! I was bullied from second grade to eighth grade. It was awful. Kids made fun of me, stole and vandalized my stuff, blamed me for things I didn't do (groups of kids ganged up and told a teacher I had). I always feared what would happen next. And I was forced to be in this environment, school, for about forty hours a week for seven years. SEVEN YEARS...

It only stopped when I got good at something. I was a rockstar soccer goalie in high school. Yes, a rockstar. I set all the school records in stats—still hold them. I was team captain, defensive MVP, team MVP, first team all-conference, all-state, and played in the all-state all-star game. Colleges recruited me to play for them. And I leaned into this. Hard. I became a cocky, arrogant a**hole. I didn't know how to handle feeling wanted, being the best in an area. After seven years of torment, I was super high on myself. I never bullied, though—hell no. I stood up to the bullies and took the bullied under my wing. But I thought my sh*t didn't stink and I could do whatever I wanted. I yelled at my coach in the middle of a game: "Coach, shut up!" He knew he couldn't take me out because I was too good at my role. He literally said that to me at halftime.

I am not this way anymore, even though I bragged about myself a moment ago. I have spectacular friends who make sure my head doesn't get too big, keep me in check, and bring me back to Earth if I ever feel a little too out of this world. Thanks, inner circle!

I didn't end up playing soccer in college. None of the recruiting colleges had engineering. Instead, I went to a college that did and tried out for the team. I had the absolute worst tryout of my life. Oh man, was I awful. I was getting nutmegged (where they score the goal by shooting it between my legs). In retrospect, I see that this was the best thing that could have happened. If I had made the team, I would not have dedicated myself so much to my studies and my dreams of becoming a NASA Rocket Scientist. I would have prioritized practice and team bonding. Lots of the guys who did make the team changed their major from engineering to something easier to be able to do both. Thanks, Coach Enzo, for cutting me.

Back to that NASA Rocket Scientist dream. I grew up in a small town in Wisconsin with about eleven thousand residents. They laughed when I said I wanted to work for NASA. Even in college, parents of my friends would chuckle when I told them about my goal of being a Rocket Scientist for NASA. People put limits on me. On my beliefs. On my dreams. They didn't understand. They were surprised and reacted with disbelief. I didn't let them, or ANYTHING, stop me.

It took me three years and more than 150 applications before I got my first NASA internship during undergrad. While there, I realized I needed to get an advanced degree if I really wanted a shot at a full-time job. So after a lot of research I decided Georgia Tech was the perfect place for me, so I applied. However, Georgia Tech initially rejected my application to grad school, but three weeks later I fought to get accepted and also got myself a graduate research assistantship, which paid for my tuition and gave me a stipend for living expenses. Next, I set my sights on NASA JPL. Nearing graduation from Georgia Tech, I went through three rounds of interviews only to not be hired. I was a few months from graduation here, so I graduated without a full-time job but got myself a ten-week temporary internship from a mentor I was doing graduate research with. He believed in me and said, "Once I get you here, it's your job to prove to them you belong." I like to say that if I was unsuccessful, I'd either have to move back home to live with my parents or become a beach bum in Los Angeles, but in my mind there really was no plan B, so I got to work. I set up over thirty interviews for myself in the last five weeks after hitting the ground running with work. I was just about to ask for an internship extension on my last day when I was offered a full-time position as a NASA JPL Systems Engineer. I was officially a real Rocket Scientist.

Woohoo! Goal accomplished. What a journey.

So then, why did I quit?

Wait, what? Kevin, you quit your dream job?

Yep. Why did I fire NASA and go off to do my own thing after I worked so hard to achieve that?

It's now been about four years since I left NASA, and my understanding of that experience has evolved and deepened. I tried to go back and look at some past journal entries and my last book, but none of the words I found could accurately describe it in the detail I feel today. So here ya go, you get a fresh look at Why I Left NASA (tears may or may not have been shed while writing this part...).

For the first six months I was ecstatic. I was living the dream every single day. Sunny Los Angeles, the beach on the weekends, and designing spaceships during the week. Each time I walked onto the campus I was like, "F*ck yeah, I did it!" However, I soon saw that life at NASA JPL, and outside of work, was not exactly what I had envisioned. I got there, and after the initial excitement wore off, I began to think, "Hmmm, this doesn't fill my soul like I thought it would."

The novelty wore off, and I started to experience things that didn't sit right with me. Things like an increasing lack of transparency from HR and the executive board; management trying to put two people into a cubicle that was too small for one person; being forced to work on projects I didn't like (auditing of assessments, boring, but I did win an award for my work on it); being at a computer in a cubicle all day; lower pay than my private-space industry counterparts; time-based promotions (rather than merit-based); and restrictions on outside activities.

I've compared it to a party you're looking forward to, you're super excited, you buy a new outfit, tell all your friends about it...but then you get to the party, and the party sucks. If it's just a party, you leave and look for a new party. But I couldn't just leave, I had bills to pay. I was an adult now, fully responsible for my own life.

That last part, "restrictions on outside activities," meant that I had to get everything I wanted to do approved by the ethics office. From being a certified personal trainer to competing on *American Ninja Warrior*, they had the final say in if I could do that or not. Hmmm—that doesn't feel right.

Did I just need to find my place within NASA? Did I need to accept that this was life and make the best of it? NO. Two incidents really solidified my realization that I needed to leave. The first was reading Lewis Howes's book *The School of Greatness*. He listed the habits of the richest individuals in the world. As I read through that list I thought, "Umm, I do every single one of these, no joke, but there is no way to increase my income within NASA. I could never be one of those rich people rewarded substantially for their efforts." Do I do side hustles to make more money? Yes, but that still doesn't change my reality of working forty–sixty hours a week in a cubicle, trading time for money.

The second story is the one that really hit my soul, hit it deep, like an impactor. (That's a spacecraft that we intentionally crash into the surface of something to expose subsurface material—we literally impact the surface to create a crater.) We threw a retirement party for my boss's boss. He gave a speech in which he said, "Now I can finally live my life the way I want. I can wake up when I want, I can go to bed when I want, I can go wherever I want." He looked like he was having the happiest day of his life. He's retiring...he's like sixty-five...yet he can't go outside without a hat on because of a condition.... Whoa. Dude, I'm twenty-five years old at this party, and you're telling me I have to wait forty years to feel that way? That I have to "pay my dues" to live my life the way I want when I don't even have much life or health left? OH, HELLS TO THE NO. Nope, this is not the life path for me.

So that's the dirt, the tea, it's been spilt. I had worked for fifteen years to prepare myself to achieve and crush it at my dream job. Every decision I made, from summer school to choosing a minor to grad school to speaking to mentors, I made so I could succeed at NASA and climb the ranks there. And now I was doing just that. I was killing it. I won awards. I was a rockstar all around. I saw how everything worked and is connected science-wise/politically/ business-wise. I really "got it" at NASA. People were telling me I could be the director someday if I really wanted it. But here's the thing…I didn't want it. I couldn't find a single person at NASA JPL who made me think, "I want your job." None of their lives appealed to me anymore. It was all so restrictive, too structured, not enough freedom.

So what did I do? I knew I needed to make money some other way so I could leave NASA. I explored so many options: for example, a fitness clothing company, a model spacecraft company, online personal training, health and fitness YouTube videos. I read Tim Ferris's *4-Hour Work Week* and tried a bunch of methods he suggested. I started reading a book a week, hoping to find golden nuggets of information that would grant me access to my freedom. If I just do X, I thought, then I'm golden! But I couldn't find X. I failed at all of them.

Well, I don't believe in failure. I believe in giving up or succeeding, so I gave up on all of them that weren't getting me returns. Only when I looked inward did I discover what would work.

At NASA I fell in love with public outreach. I was the most active member of the NASA JPL Speakers Bureau. During my lunches, my evenings, and my weekends I went to schools, libraries, symposiums—any event—and spoke about space. Heck, I even took vacation days to go out and spread the good word of science. I fell IN LOVE with educating people about space.

Some people at NASA tried to put limits on my space-education efforts, from the ethics office to my boss's boss. They tried telling me what to say, how to say it, when to say it, where I couldn't say it, what I could do, what I couldn't do. They didn't want me to educate or present myself in modern ways or as much as I was doing. They tried to hold me back from achieving my goals of bringing space down to Earth: to expose, educate, and inspire as many people as possible about the wonders of space exploration and its importance to us here on Earth.

My mantra was "don't ask for permission, beg for forgiveness," and I really leaned into being a public-space expert. I tried to work with NASA, but there was too much red tape and internal politics holding me back, and one person in particular who wanted to prevent me from doing this work. I did it anyway. I started to build up some gigs and get some exposure. If I was representing NASA, I couldn't make money. But as a "Georgia Tech–educated aerospace engineer working in the space industry" I could. However, I needed to leap. If I left NASA, I could use NASA to promote myself. I could let everyone know I was a NASA Rocket Scientist.

CHAPTER TWO

Disruptors and Famous Launchers

Here's to the crazy ones, the misfits, the rebels, the troublemakers, the round pegs in the square holes... the ones who see things differently—they're not fond of rules.... You can quote them, disagree with them, glorify or vilify them, but the only thing you can't do is ignore them because they change things...they push the human race forward, and while some may see them as the crazy ones, we see genius, because the ones who are crazy enough to think that they can change the world, are the ones who do.
–STEVE JOBS, 1997

So... I QUIT. I...quit...NASA.

Yep. I quit the job I dreamed of having since I was ten years old. The one that took me fifteen years and hundreds of rejections to achieve. I quit NASA to start my own space-education and consulting company, to be a public-space expert.

I cried every single day after giving my notice. Was I doing the right thing? Giving up my dream job? Quitting NASA? No, Kevin, I told myself, you didn't quit. You *fired* NASA because it was holding YOU back from becoming the best version of yourself! And yes,

I wholeheartedly believe that was the right decision, but damn, it took a while to actually feel that in my soul. I went against society, against logic, against the grain. I was doing the unthinkable.

But you know what? So did so many other people. There was literally a wall highlighting them in my office building, Building 301, with the word DISRUPTORS in between all their headshots. That stared me in the face every single day. Teasing me, luring me in. Whispering to me, "Kevin, you are a Disruptor, you have to do it, you have no choice."

Join that wall, Kevin. Do it.

Many people have called me crazy for quitting NASA, and you might even be one of them. That's okay—this is my path, you have yours.

That wall showed me concrete examples of the possibilities of going against the status quo. The people who worked in Building 301 were a part of the three Advanced Design Engineering teams (A-Team, TeamX, and TeamXc). NASA's intent was to inspire us to do things that have never been done before, to create designs that were out of this world, but they didn't expect to inspire me to put NASA in the rearview mirror. Every single day showing me examples through history of individuals and technologies that defied limits and disrupted existing conditions, highlighting the fact that even in the face of worldwide adversity and stubbornness, one can break through the noise and create change. A lot of these individuals, just like me, were laughed at. Many of these people came from a broken state. However, those individuals were geniuses—they were the crazy ones who actually changed the world.

May the **Disruptors** also open your eyes to the possibilities that are out there and break the notion that things thought to be impossible really are.

The Disruptors

The Disruptors (left-to-right): Autonomous Vehicle, Tony Hawk, Wright brothers, Prince, Sputnik, Steve Jobs, Johannes Kepler, Mars Cube One, Carl Sagan, Magic Johnson, Oprah Winfrey, Lady Gaga, Alan Turing, Marie Curie, Captain James Cook, Chuck Berry, Grace Hopper, Mars Helicopter, Additive Manufacturing, Voyager, Pelé, Orson Welles, Benjamin Franklin, David Bowie, Kirobo Robo-naut

Autonomous Vehicle: Self-driving cars, removing the human factor from driving a car to improve traffic flow and safety on the road.

Tony Hawk: Legendary skateboarder who created his own brand of tricks and was the first ever to land a 900 as well as twelve straight world championship titles.

Wright brothers: First to achieve powered flight, from bicycle makers to pilots, on December 17, 1903, in Kitty Hawk, North Carolina.

Prince: Singer-songwriter and multi-instrumentalist who brought a new wave of music mixing funk, rock, and pop and crushed the bland masculine stereotype by displaying androgynous sexuality.

Sputnik: First artificial satellite launched by the Soviet Union in 1957, which marked the start of the Space Race, sparking the creation of NASA.

Steve Jobs: Apple cofounder, pioneer of the personal computer and music player industry.

Johannes Kepler: Astronomer, best known for his laws of planetary motion proving that the planets traveled in elliptical orbits around the sun and that their speed is related to the radius of the planet's orbit.

Mars Cube One: First pair of interplanetary cubesats that launched with NASA Mars InSight lander and provided real-time data of InSight's landing on Mars.

Carl Sagan: Astronomer, planetary scientist, cosmologist, astrophysicist, astrobiologist, author, and science communicator. Known by many to be the first true space popularist, inspiring countless individuals and the original host and creator of Cosmos with his wife, Ann Druyan.

Magic Johnson: NBA player (said by some to be the greatest point guard of all time) and HIV advocate, creator of the Magic John Foundation to combat HIV.

Oprah Winfrey: Talk show host, TV producer, actress, author, and philanthropist.

Lady Gaga: Singer, songwriter, and actress who reshaped the music industry with her discography encompassing all genres and styles as well as outrageous performances touting her personal flair.

Alan Turning: Mathematician, computer scientist, developed the idea for the Universal Turing Machine, which is the basis for the first computer, and created the test for AI in 1950 that is still used today.

Marie Curie: Physicist and chemist pioneering radioactivity work, where she discovered polonium and radium and championed the use of radiation in medicine and fundamentally changed our understanding of radioactivity.

Captain James Cook: British explorer famous for his three voyages between 1768 and 1779 in the Pacific Ocean, and to New Zealand and Australia in particular.

Chuck Berry: Singer, songwriter, and guitarist who pioneered rock and roll and wrote the famous song "Johnny B Goode," which is used in the *Back to the Future* movie and is on the Golden Record of the Voyager spacecraft.

Grace Hopper: Computer scientist, one of the first programmers of the Harvard Mark I computer, a pioneer of computer programming who invented one of the first linkers or computer program compiler.

Mars Helicopter: First powered flight on another planet launched and landed with NASA Mars Perseverance rover on February 18, 2021.

Additive Manufacturing: Process that allows three-dimensional objects to be printed from digital data allowing instantaneous creation of tools or other objects.

Voyager: First interstellar twin probes launched in 1977, still operating in the year 2022. Voyager 2 is the only spacecraft to date to visit Uranus and Neptune.

Pelé: A Brazilian soccer legend known to be the best player of all time. He played for the New York Cosmos after he retired and really brought soccer into the mainstream for the American public.

Orson Welles: Director, actor, screenwriter, and producer remembered for his innovative work in radio, theater, and film.

Benjamin Franklin: Writer, scientist, inventor, statesman, diplomat, printer, publisher, and political philosopher.

David Bowie: Singer-songwriter and actor with the stage name Ziggy Stardust, who predicted the digital evolution of the music industry. He also brought a dramatic sense of showmanship and theatricality to rock music.

Kirobo Robo-naut: Japan's first robot astronaut designed to work in zero-gravity and assist in experiments, which arrived at the International Space Station on August 10, 2013, accompanying the first Japanese Commander Koichi Wakata.

The Disruptors wall was reimagined by Tony Freeman, the program manager for JPL's Innovation Foundry. I spoke to him about the concept for the wall and how it came to be. Tony said that the new Disruptors wall was an updated version of the original one, which was heavy on the early twentieth century, mostly male artists like Salvador Dali and Picasso, and had become quite dated. I wanted to know how the Disruptors were chosen for the new wall. It turns out that the process for coming up with the new wall wasn't exactly scientific. Tony said that the individuals who were included had to have disrupted their field of endeavor, but they couldn't be present-day space pioneers. His group polled people at JPL and friends and relatives, asking for suggestions about people they would like to include. Some of Tony's own personal heroes included on the wall were Captain James Cook and David Bowie, and to a degree Alan Turing because of his connection to Manchester (Tony's alma mater). "We wanted a diverse population, so that JPLers from all kinds of backgrounds could relate to the people featured. The physical objects were representative of things that changed the world and had a space relevance."

The genius behind the implementation of this wall installation is David Levine, a Creative and Visual Strategist at NASA Jet Propulsion Laboratory and founder of a creative design company called Loved Observed. His work has been featured at cultural events and museums globally including the Museum of Modern Art, the Grammys, Super Bowl, Tribeca Film Festival, E3, MTV Music Awards, U.S. Open, CES, NASCAR, Sundance Film Festival, New York Fashion Week, and the Brooklyn Bridge Anchorage. As a member of the JPL Design Studio, he works with scientists and engineers to inspire and communicate the brilliance behind NASA JPL's missions, helping with everything from concepting mission artwork to creating immersive art installations like the Disruptors wall.

The Disruptors wall inspired me every day I walked into Building 301. It also got me thinking about another category of innovator:

Famous Launchers. A Disruptor causes radical change by means of innovation. A Famous Launcher is someone who has made their dream come true by defying overwhelming odds. Disruptors show you that radical change is possible against the status quo. Famous Launchers show you that goals can be accomplished in the face of adversity.

Note that a **Disruptor** *is a* **Famous Launcher,** *but a* **Famous Launcher** *is not necessarily a* **Disruptor.**

Let's get into some examples of what I'm talking about, because who doesn't appreciate some inspiration?

For the first deep dive I want to start with the most dramatic example of a **Famous Launcher**, the most impactful, the author of my favorite book—the book that grounds me and shows me the way. Each time I've read Viktor Frankl's *Man's Search for Meaning* has proven to be a pivotal time in my life, either reaffirming my direction or setting me on a new course. Frankl was a holocaust survivor and psychologist, the creator of logotherapy. At the time of his death in 1997, his book had sold over ten million copies and been translated into twenty-four languages. If you haven't read it, go buy it right now. Put my book down and purchase his. I'll be here when you get back :).

Buuuuut for those of you who won't, or who already have read it, let's recap. Viktor Frankl was imprisoned at several concentration camps by Nazis, including Auschwitz. His wife and family were killed by the Nazis. His book is broken up into two parts, the first describing his time in the concentration camps and the second describing logotherapy. Viktor made it through the literal worst of humanity and then used that experience to help millions. He initially was going to publish his concentration camp stories anonymously but decided to go public and share his personal experiences with the world.

He was at the lowest of low. Death for him may have been better than what he went through. And yet, he felt a purpose behind *why* he had to make it through: to share his logotherapy with the world. He saw its importance firsthand in the, again, literal worst of humanity. I can't describe it any other way. Viktor gave his suffering a meaning, and that is what part of logotherapy is about: "He who has a *why* to live can bear almost any how," he wrote. This quote sums up the whole book and logotherapy (the school of psychology Frankl developed).

"Everything can be taken from a man but one thing: the last of the human freedoms—to choose one's attitude in any given set of circumstances, to choose one's own way," he wrote. And you're going to need that mindset on your journey. That's so critical. The journey is difficult, whether you're launching yourself into the next level of your life or just getting through this one. Your attitude is everything. If Viktor Frankl can make it through his life experience and come out unjaded, you can do anything. Someone always has it harder than you. How's that for perspective?

Your attitude is your launch pad. It is the foundation, the sturdy base in which everything is placed on top of. It's the starting block for everything that follows, from the NASA Design Levels to The Practices. Right now, your attitude might need some adjustments, possibly a large paradigm shift, or just a minor tune-up. That's why you've picked up this book in the first place. You want to learn something new, and any new information contributes to a shift in attitude.

Attitude is not constant; it will vary as you go through life. There will be moments of strength, when you have a fortified attitude and truly embody the Phoenix Mentality. And there will be moments of weakness, when you feel sad, let down, rejected, possibly depressed or broken. The key here is that you do not sit in the moments of weakness, but learn to shift yourself from low to neutral to high mentally. Even in the lows of life, you can have an optimistic attitude that gets you through them and out of them.

That attitude is what will allow you to walk the path of the NASA Design Levels. If you approach them with a poor attitude, you will get poor results. As computer coders like to say, "Garbage in, garbage out." So, turn the mindset switch to the positive side, turn its dial from bad to good, and let's put those Levels into play in your life. Need help flipping the switch, turning the dial? Your answer lives in Part 3—The Practices. You might find it advantageous to read through this whole book and then go back through Part 2— The Process to revisit the NASA Design Levels with a new attitude incorporating The Practices.

Each Disruptor and Famous Launcher had to embody Frankl's idea about attitude as a foundational block for everything that followed. Breaking through the wall of normalcy, of the current reality, definitely came with ridicule, laughter, doubters, and haters. To succeed in this environment requires control of one's mindset. The Disruptors and Famous Launchers, like you, needed to hold strong in adverse conditions, ignore the haters, and not react to the masses casting doubt on their ideas.

I had never heard of Martine Rothblatt until early 2022, when I heard Lewis Howes interview her on *The School of Greatness* podcast. I was running at the time, but her story was so amazing I stopped and wrote her name in my phone notes so I could go back and do an even deeper dive on her. I learned that Martine Rothblatt is an American lawyer, author, entrepreneur, and transgender rights advocate who said, "I'm a person who likes to hear why something can't be done and I'll whittle down every one of the can'ts one at a time."

You've definitely heard of her first company: she cofounded Sirius Satellite Radio in 1990. Yeah, that's amazing, *but* that's not what this story is about. At age forty, Rothblatt underwent sex reassignment surgery and, in 1994, publicly identified for the first time as transgender. She has become a vocal advocate for transgender rights and has led efforts to establish appropriate health-law standards for the transgender community and to resist discriminatory legislation. Again amazing, *but* that's not what this story is about, either.

In 1995, her seven-year-old daughter Jenesis was diagnosed with an incurable and deadly disease, primary pulmonary hypertension (PPH). Doctors only gave her a few years to live. Rothblatt did not accept "incurable" as a fact. She went down the wormhole in biology to learn everything she could about PPH and created the PPH Cure Foundation. She even took a doctoral course in medical ethics at St. Bartholomew's Hospital in London. She was frustrated with the slow pace of a search for a cure, so she founded a new medical biotech company in 1996 called United Therapeutics. Just a few years later, that company developed Orenitram to treat PPH and save Jenesis's life. Now United Therapeutics sells five FDA-approved drugs to help people with the disease and has created a treatment for neuroblastoma, a cancer that most often arises in the adrenal glands.

The experts told Martine that Jenesis was going to die in a few years due to an incurable disease. She, as no one would, didn't like that answer and decided that it was *not* the answer. That the experts were wrong. She set off to change the impossible to possible, driven by the love for her daughter. Martine's **Why** was rooted in the strongest emotion of them all—love. Not only did she disrupt the medical industry around PPH, but she did so in an incredibly short time frame. Medical treatments for disease usually take several years to come to success. That timeline can be shorter with increased resources, as with COVID-19, when the entire world worked to develop a vaccine. SARS-CoV-2, the virus that causes COVID-19, was first identified in December 2019. By December 11, 2020, the Pfizer vaccine became the first to receive emergency use authorization from the Food and Drug Administration (FDA). But Martine did not have the entire world helping or a global pandemic breathing down all around her to fast-track her medical research. She was fueled by the love for her daughter and the attitude of "nothing is impossible."

How does someone like Martine do such things? Why don't they give up? What ignites them to try in the first place? When things don't go right, how do they know what to do to keep going? Do they have a process that you can model so that you can achieve similar feats?

Yes.

That's half of the core information you'll get out of this book: the NASA Design Levels. Even if they don't call it that, people like Martine use a process, consciously or unconsciously, that's the same process I used to design spacecraft with NASA. Life seems hard because it actually is rocket science too. When designing out-of-this-world vehicles, we're creating something that has never been created before to do something that's never been done…literally. It makes sense that the Disruptors and Famous Launchers, the change authoritarians and goal seekers, also use the same process. They're trying to do things that have never been done before. What better structure to model off of than NASA, the organization that's trying to answer questions that we don't have answers to?

The other half of the core information is The Practices, which forge your Phoenix Mentality. I will address this fully in Part 3, but I'll highlight some of the practices displayed by Famous

Launchers as we take them through the NASA Design Levels in Part 2. Before we move into Parts 2 and 3, I'd like to tell you about some major lifestyle and societal changes that people either fought against or deemed impossible. From some of the world's brightest minds to large institutions, doubters and close-minded thinkers are everywhere. I'm sharing these stories in the next chapter to show you concrete examples of defying limitations to implement change and advance our world.

CHAPTER THREE
Defying Limits
Throughout History

Somewhere, something incredible is waiting to be known.
–CARL SAGAN

THROUGHOUT HISTORY THERE have been so many examples of impossible turned possible. Crazy turned ordinary. The unthinkable becoming habit. And the process for all of these follows the same basic structure: the NASA Design Levels. The structure that I used to explore thirty-plus advanced space mission concepts with NASA JPL's advanced design engineering teams: A-Team, TeamX, and TeamXc. We'll launch into the NASA Design Levels in Part 2—The Process, but first let's break some status quos with concepts and technologies that reshaped society. These stories show you that dramatic change is possible even in the face of doubt from large institutions and the brightest minds of the time.

Some Disruptors may not even see their work come to fruition in their lifetimes. And they definitely couldn't have done it alone. They all had teams behind them. For Martine Rothblatt, it was all the employees at her company. For Viktor Frankl, it was the other inmates in the concentration camps, then later friends and publishers. If you are a Disruptor or end up becoming one, amazing, you are truly incredible. But I'm not telling you that you need to be one. I'm setting you up to be a Launcher, not even necessarily a Famous Launcher. You can if you want to be, but what I'm going to show is that with these Disruptor individuals, disruptive technology, and Famous Launchers, the fundamental process to become each one starts with the NASA Design Levels and The Practices to make you a Launcher. That is your cornerstone, or more appropriate for this book, your launching pad.

Each change or goal starts with an idea: it's believed to be possible by its originator, they explore how it could be done, they choose a way to do it, they try it. If it works, great. But if not, they explore how it could be done again, then try a different approach. As things start to work, new challenges appear. More time, energy, and other resources are put in, and doubters continue to question or put obstacles in the way. Then more obstacles yet. This is the process of achieving dreams, and it is the process for designing spaceships. Before we even talk about space, we gotta bring ourselves down to Earth. All the way, not in the sky, down to the ground. To the things that get us from A to B most often. Nope, not our legs anymore—we're lazy. And for this we can thank the automobile.

The automobile got its start in 1886 as a three-wheeled motor car patented by Karl Benz. Not needing a horse to get around sounds like an idea that everyone could agree on right? Not so much. Automobiles were not seen as something everyone could agree on. Big publishers cast doubt on the autos, multiple times. "The ordinary 'horseless carriage' is at present a luxury for the wealthy; and although its price will probably fall in the future, it will never, of course, come into as common use as the bicycle," claimed the *Literary Digest* in 1899. And a few years later: "The actual building of roads devoted to motor cars is not for the near future, in spite of many rumors to that effect," wrote *Harper's Weekly*. What I really love is what Henry Ford said when asked to put into words how hard it was to sell the idea to the public: "If I had asked people what they wanted, they would have said faster horses."

Did that stop the teams moving forward to make them household items? No, it certainly didn't. Karl Benz and Henry Ford were thinkers ahead of their time. Benz didn't fit in well at any of his professional positions before he started his own factory to make inventions. Benz had ideas, believed he could do them, thought of different ways, tried one, and then failed. His first business was confiscated by the authorities, due to an unreliable business partner. So he started again, this time a little differently, and eventually introduced the *Benz Patent Motorwagen*.

Okay, now that we've hit the ground running, or rolling, we can take off. Time for the airplane. In 1895 Thomas Edison said, "The possibilities of the aeroplane have been exhausted and we must turn elsewhere." That same year, the British mathematician, physicist, and engineer Lord Kelvin, who invented the Kelvin temperature scale, said, "I can state flatly that heavier-than-air flying machines are impossible." A mere eight years later, on December 17, 1903, the Wright brothers had their first flight at Kitty Hawk. And look at us now! Some of the brightest minds of the nineteenth century put limits on a concept, saying it was impossible. Those limits were broken. Not only do we have heavier-than-air flying machines, we have an Antonov An-225 Mriya airplane, which can weigh 640 tonnes at takeoff, and we have sent people into outer space. Speaking of outer space...

On January 13, 1920, the *New York Times* proclaimed that space flight was impossible because there was nothing in the cosmic void for the exhaust to push against.[4] They said that Professor Robert H. Goddard, who today is considered the father of modern rocket propulsion, "lacks the knowledge ladled out daily in high schools."

On July 17, 1969, the day after Apollo 11's launch, the *New York Times* issued a correction:

A Correction

On Jan. 13, 1920, "Topics of The Times," an editorial-page feature of The New York Times, dismissed the notion that a rocket could function in a vacuum and commented on the ideas of Robert H. Goddard, the rocket pioneer, as follows:

"That Professor Goddard, with his 'chair' in Clark College and the countenancing of the Smithsonian Institution, does not know the relation of action to reaction, and of the need to have something better than a vacuum against which to react—to say that would be absurd. Of course he only seems to lack the knowledge ladled out daily in high schools."

Further investigation and experimentation have confirmed the findings of Isaac Newton in the 17th Century and it is now definitely established that a rocket can function in a vacuum as well as in an atmosphere. The Times regrets the error.

On Jan. 13, 1920, "Topics of The Times," an editorial-page feature of The New York Times, dismissed the notion that a rocket could function in a vacuum and commented on the ideas of Robert H. Goddard, the rocket pioneer, as follows. "That Professor Goddard, with his 'chair' in Clark College and the countenancing of the Smithsonian Institution, does not know the relation of action to reaction, and of the need to have something better than a vacuum against which to react—to say that would be absurd. Of course he only seems to lack the knowledge ladled out daily in high schools." Further investigation and experimentation have confirmed the findings of Isaac Newton in the 17th century and it is now definitely established that a rocket can function in a vacuum as well as in an atmosphere. The Times regrets the error.

Three days later, Neil Armstrong and Buzz Aldrin landed on the moon while Michael Collins orbited in the command module. To date we've had over twenty-one years of continual human presence in outer space. We're constantly achieving the impossible with space travel.

If I asked you who is the smartest person in history, who comes to mind? It might just be our friendly patent office examiner Albert Einstein. He predicted many a thing well before we actually had the scientific data to prove it. Like gravitational waves in 1916, for example—which were confirmed in 2015. But he wasn't always

Einstein-y. On December 29, 1934, he was quoted in the *Pittsburgh Post-Gazette* saying, "There is not the slightest indication that [nuclear energy] will ever be obtainable. It would mean that the atom would have to be shattered at will." Hmmm, I think we achieved this. A few times. Early on and very destructively with the atom bomb in 1945. Prior to the first test explosion Fleet Admiral William Leahy allegedly told President Truman, "This is the biggest fool thing we've ever done—the bomb will never go off—and I speak as an expert on explosives." Eventually we harnessed the nuclear reaction in a safe fashion, and in 1954 the USSR became the first country to supply some of its electricity with its Obninsk nuclear power plant.

We at NASA (yes, I will always say "we" when referring to NASA even though I left in 2018) use nuclear energy to power spacecrafts that are billions of miles away. Kilometers, I mean billions of kilometers. We rarely use English units such as miles in space exploration. We launched, and continue to launch, nuclear reactors into outer space. Yeah, we strapped a nuclear reactor to a fifty-three-ton bomb, the Thor-DM21 Able-Star rocket, in 1961 when we launched the U.S. Navy's Transit IV satellite, the first nuclear-powered spacecraft.

Our scientific community has gotten pretty good at obtaining nuclear energy. In 1977 we (yes, NASA again) launched the twin Voyager probes that would become the furthest traveling human made objects. Both were powered by a radioisotope thermoelectric generator (RTG), which is a type of nuclear battery that harnesses the heat coming off decaying radioactive material and turns that into electricity for the spacecraft. The Voyagers are *still* operating today (as I write this on July 19, 2022) and will for a bit longer.

So despite doubters like Albert Einstein, we obtained nuclear energy, made it into bombs, and strapped it to bombs as we sent it to space. Those power plants continue to work forty-five years later without any maintenance, billions of miles away. At this moment of writing Voyager 2 is 14,537,290,721 miles from Earth, and as I wrote that, it's already inaccurate because the craft is traveling at 38,026.77 mph. Check out the current positions and speeds of both the Voyagers at *https://voyager.jpl.nasa.gov/mission/status/.*

We've gotten bigger, faster, and farther so far. Let's bring it back down to Earth for our next example. Let's get small—let's go quantum! Nahhh, not that small, but something that definitely seemed as absurd as quantum mechanics at the time. In 2001 Steve Jobs pulled a device from his pocket and said, "A thousand songs in your pocket," to pitch the first iPod to the world. People said, "What? Impossible!"

Music was stored on CDs (compact discs), which maxed out at about one hundred minutes of music, or early MP3 players, which at first held only eight or nine songs. For an average song length of three minutes, that's only thirty-three songs on a CD. Steve Jobs was pitching a thirty-times increase in capacity. The first MP3 player to hold more than twenty songs at a time was the Remote Solutions Personal Jukebox (PJB-100), released in the fall of 1999. He was pitching an increase in capacity and decrease in size for MP3s. People thought he must have figured out how to break the laws of physics! Not crazy if you understand Moore's Law.

Moore's Law refers to Gordon Moore's insight that, thanks to technological advances, the number of transistors on a microchip doubles every two years as the cost of computers is halved. Moore's Law states that we can expect the speed and capability of our computers to increase every couple of years, and we will pay less for them. Basically, when we refer to Moore's Law, we say that advancements in technology in general double every two years. It compounds upon itself, like compound interest in the financial world. If you don't know what that is, oh my, it has the power to make you rich! Go learn about that and invest now. Do it. Put this book down, Google "compound interest," and then come back tomorrow and continue reading.

Moore's Law was based on historical trends, so it's not a true law like we have in physics, but more of an empirical relationship linked to gains from experience in production. Today we say that Moore's Law is still delivering exponential improvements in all aspects of the world. We're learning and growing faster than ever before. This is excellent, because we are in the age of technology and global connection. We can create businesses from our smartphones with just our fingertips. The possibilities for you are endless, whatever your goals. Products and concepts exist today that were thought impossible just a few decades ago. We're lucky to be alive at this time, when we have the options available to us to pursue whatever dreams interest us. And we have access to all the information possible to allow us to achieve them. Let's take a peek into the music industry to see how far we've come in that technology arena, to open our eyes to what changes and advancements are possible in a short period of time.

For music player technology, we'll start with the 33 RPM 12-inch record in 1948 from Columbia Records. In 1963 the compact cassette tape was introduced by the Phillips company. This is basically the same technology NASA JPL used on the Galileo spacecraft launched in 1989 to record its data: a magnetic tape recorder. In 1964 there was this thing called an 8-track tape. And in 1982 the compact disc, aka the CD, arrived (which might be the only one you've heard of before if you're younger than me). Then, in 1992, the first MP3 player came out, which only held eight or nine songs, rising to one thousand songs in 2001 with the iPod. Now we have infinite access to streaming services like Spotify and YouTube, endless access to all songs from our device…

that also happens to make phone calls...with video...to anyone, anywhere, anytime. Wow, we're literally living a science-fiction reality right now.

Steve Jobs is both a Disruptor and a Famous Launcher who fully exemplifies the NASA Design Levels. Did you know that Steve Jobs was forced out from Apple, the company he started in 1976 with Steve Wozniak, in 1985? It wasn't until 1997, twelve years later, that Jobs returned to Apple. He came in with the "Think Different" campaign and, boom, the iPod launched in 2001. Jobs's story shows that you could achieve that dream of yours and then have it taken away from you. But that's not the end. There is never an end unless you stop trying. There is no failure; there is giving up or succeeding. You have to keep pressing on until you make it happen. Just as in the NASA Design Levels, Steve Jobs had to figure out a different approach to his idea and then have a go at it again.

One more anecdote on advancing technology with Moore's Law that can turn your dreams into reality: the *Star Wars* movies. The first six movies were released in this order: 4, 5, 6, 1, 2, 3. Doesn't seem to make much sense, does it? Why would the fourth movie be the first to be released? Well, that is because George Lucas had ideas for movies 1, 2, and 3 that would require technology that didn't exist at the time: "I had Yoda, but he couldn't fight. I had cities, but I couldn't build models that big. I had lots and lots of costumes, but I couldn't afford to make them. So there were a lot of issues that were just practical—Episode I wasn't doable for a long time, so I waited until we had the technology to do it."[5] He wanted to make those movies with the technology that would be available in the future, so he tucked them away, waiting for the tools he'd need to realize his dream of making those films astonishing on the silver screen.

I could highlight more and more of these instances, and I will in the following chapters with some specific people to serve as role models who employed NASA's Design Levels unknowingly. But to close this one out I'll leave you with a quote from news reporter and editor Nick Whigham on August 1, 2016, in his article titled "The Life Changing Inventions the Experts Said Were Impossible":[6]

> From Lord Kelvin's boast that "X-rays will prove to be a hoax" to Astronomer Forest Moulton's assertion that "there is no hope for the fanciful idea of reaching the moon because of insurmountable barriers to escaping the Earth's gravity," there has been plenty of incidents in the past that illustrate the hazards of scientific prophecy—especially when it comes to the doubters.

If the innovations I've described have been implemented on a global scale, whatever thoughts you may have are definitely possible. The evidence speaks for itself; nothing is impossible. So let's get to work on bringing you to a higher orbit and making your dreams a reality. The content of this book will show you how to be a launcher in your own life. To gain confidence and motivation. To face adversity and come out on top. To figure out your vision, put a plan in place, and take action on it. To build up a Phoenix Mentality so that you can weather any storm that comes your way.

Part 1—The Proof

Part 2—The Process

Part 3—The Practices

CHAPTER FOUR

NASA Design Levels

*NASA is an engine of innovation and inspiration as well
as the world's premier space exploration agency.*
—BILL NYE

NASA JPL HAS advanced design engineering groups called
A-Team, TeamX, and TeamXc. These groups focus on innovation
formulation with creative thinkers and subject-matter experts.
I was a part of these three teams for a few years, led a lot of the
organization, and even helped develop TeamXc (which is basically
TeamX for cubesats, which are small modular satellites).

A-Team operates out of a room called "Left Field" because
the craziest ideas come out of left field. Picture wall-to-wall
whiteboards, bright colors, beanbag chairs, craft supplies, overhead
projectors, giant flat-screen monitors, and LEGOs. Reminiscent
of a kindergarten classroom, this space fosters creativity among
world experts in space exploration—the best of the best of Rocket
Scientists, if you will. It's a nursery for space exploration mission
concepts. Things like the Mars rover Skycrane were born out of this
space. This is the birds and the bees of space concepts.

TeamX and TeamXc are where the technological powerhouses
are then thrown at the space concepts. These are separate rooms
with rows and rows of computers, one for each expert in a certain

discipline, all linked up via a custom intranet for integrating and iterating computational models. Experts in this room come from areas such as cost, systems engineering, instruments, science, trajectory, propulsion, attitude determination and control, telecommunications, ground systems, command and data handling, flight software, assembly, test and launch operations, thermal, electrical power system, mechanical, and 3D modeling. Straight from the NASA website: "TeamX is a cross-functional multidisciplinary team of engineers that utilizes concurrent engineering methodologies to complete rapid design, analysis and evaluation of mission concept designs. This advanced design team of experienced flight-project engineers is co-located in the Project Design Center to complete architecture, mission, and instrument design studies in real time."[7]

I participated in over thirty different space mission concepts and spacecraft design studies. We call each project a "study," and they can last from a single three-hour session to a few weeks at a time. I worked on things like Earth orbiters, moon sample return, Mars sample return, Enceladus (a moon of Saturn) sample return, asteroid landers, Titan (another moon of Saturn) submarines and boats, Uranus and Neptune orbiters, and telescopes looking back to the beginning of our universe and exploring exoplanets for life. This is my basis for calling myself a Space Expert in Robotic Solar System Exploration. Each one of these went through the design process I'm about to walk you through.

Day in and day out for years, this process was ingrained in me while I did it myself and walked others through it, whether they were clients coming to us to examine their space concepts or interns/new hires needing training to join the teams. However, it wasn't until I left NASA and people kept asking, "How did you become a NASA Rocket Scientist?" that the significance of the process clicked for me. The answer I was giving time and time again was modeled after the same process I've used while designing spacecrafts and missions for years.

These teams use a structure called **CMLs,** or **Concept Maturity Levels,** created in 2008 by Mark Adler of NASA JPL.[8] Throughout this book I refer to the CMLs as NASA Design Levels. For this chapter all I'm going to do is introduce the NASA Design Levels by giving a little background. For the rest of Part 2, we'll do a deep dive into each one, following one individual in particular along the way, Sylvester Stallone, and discover the secret sauce used by Famous Launchers to get through each level.

This structure was inspired by and is similar to **Technology Readiness Levels** for new spacecraft component designs. Technology Readiness Levels are a type of measurement system used to assess the maturity level of a particular technology. Basically, we ask, "Is a technology ready to be used on a mission, or is it still in development?" There are nine levels. Level 1 is the lowest, where scientific research is beginning, the idea is just born, maybe just a sketch on a piece of paper. At the top is Level 9, which means the technology has been "flight proven" during a successful mission, and it is reliable and can be used for critical missions and tasks. Think of Level 1 as a toddler being given their first basketball and Level 9 as Michael Jordan. These levels can be compared to our own life's journey too. Time to *launch* into the **NASA Design Levels**...c'mon, it's been a while since a cheesy space pun, just accept and move on.

NASA Design Level 1: Cocktail Napkin

NASA Design Level 2: Initial Feasibility

NASA Design Level 3: Trade Space

NASA Design Level 4: Point Design

NASA Design Level 5: Baseline Concept

NASA Design Level 6: Integrated Concept

NASA Design Level 7: Preliminary Implementation Baseline

NASA Design Level 8: Project Baseline

NASA Design Level 9: Implementation

IMPORTANT: For the purposes of this book, which is to give you the confidence, motivation, hope, and steps you need to achieve your dream, I want you to understand that you will only need to progress through the first five levels. Yay, five steps instead of nine! We will explore those five steps in their entirety, the core components of every space mission, every famous launcher, every dream ever achieved. Then we'll bring it home, maybe down to Earth as some say, with a discussion of refining, iterating, and never giving up.

Simple, not easy, no matter the number of steps.

I will describe briefly how all of the steps are used to do out-of-this-world things at NASA for reference and completion. First up is the standard science lingo, straight from JPL in how we defined and used the NASA Design Levels. Now I told you about the different design teams at NASA JPL. Each of the teams specializes in one or more levels of the design process. This is how NASA Design Levels are used at JPL to advance concept design maturity—that is, this is how they create a mission:

- **JPL's A-Team** (Levels 1–3): Idea generation, feasibility assessment, architecture Trade Space evaluation, science traceability, technology infusion, and strategic evaluation.
- **JPL's Team X/Xc** (Level 4): Initiated in 1995, X/Xc pioneered the collaborative engineering capability within NASA and conducted over a thousand studies on collaborative design sessions to generate a specific

mission design, spacecraft design, mission cost range, and associated risks.

- **JPL's Proposal Effort** (Levels 5–6): Enables external evaluations and costing to prepare for implementation. Top-level science requirements and mission drivers identified to derive level 2 and 3 requirements.
- **JPL's Mission Teams** (Levels 7–9): An expanding team of engineers and scientists continue to refine and elaborate on the concept by running mission scenarios with increasing fidelity.

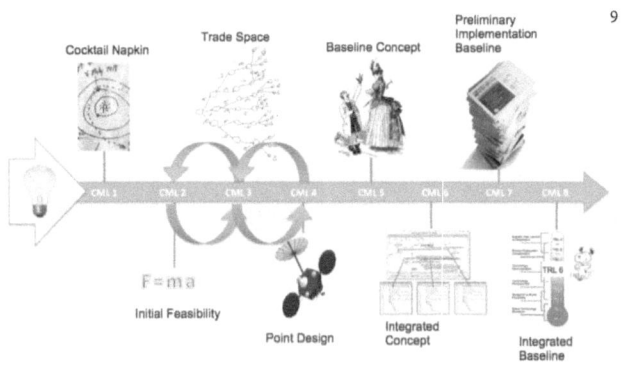

Notice here that there is a feedback loop between Levels 2, 3, and 4 in the image. It's not just a linear process, it is iterative. This is not a weakness of the NASA Design Levels but rather its strength. This feedback both allows and forces teams to revisit earlier stages of design when a problem is encountered. They can go back, modify part of the concept, and then continue on in development. This allows for getting ahead of problems early instead of finding them later down the line in the concept development process, when it could be too late to make changes, or at least make changes for a reasonable cost and effort.

Enough science and engineering corporate mumbo-jumbo, Kevin, tell me how I can use this to get what I ultimately desire in life.

Gimme the goods! Show me the money! Pull back the curtain! Unravel the mystery! All right, all right, all right, cool your rockets, strap in, and get ready for lift-off. (Yes, imagine all of that last sentence in Matthew McConaughey's voice.)

In the following chapters as we really explore what each NASA Design Level is, we'll take it step-by-step with case-study comparisons to a real NASA mission called Psyche, which is a mission to a metal asteroid; a highlight from my journey into NASA; the story of Sylvester Stallone (who'll we follow through the whole process on his journey to success); and a separate Famous Launcher case study for each level. The Psyche mission, by the way, will explore one of the most intriguing targets in the main asteroid belt: a giant metal asteroid, known as 16 Psyche, about three times farther away from the sun than is the Earth. The launch date is slated for Fall 2023.

Throughout life you will continually be challenged, especially if you are chasing your dreams, but life is about never giving up. As I've already said, there is no such thing as failure. There is succeeding, and there is giving up. There is winning or learning; there is no losing. Continue to work, to find new paths, to explore the Trade Space of Level 3 over and over again until you create the right roadmap to launch yourself and make your limitless dream a reality. Deep space exploration is up next, going down the wormhole into each NASA Design Level, picking it apart, and showing you how some of the most well-known and respected people in this world used these levels to get where they wanted to go.

CHAPTER FIVE

Level 1: Cocktail Napkin

Eureka!—I have found it!
–ARCHIMEDES

Dr. Tracy Fanara's very first job was selling rocks at eight. Then babysitting at eleven to selling cell phones at fourteen, and eventually earning her PhD from the University of Florida through sustainable design/hydrologic restoration research before going on to Mote Marine Laboratory and then the National Oceanic and Atmospheric Administration, commonly known as NOAA. Dr. Fanara set her sights on the University of Florida because of its academic reputation. She originally wanted to study oceanography, but when she went to the University of Florida they said, "No, that's Florida State," and she was extremely adamant about not going to Florida State. With her transcripts in hand, she went to every single college within the University of Florida until she found someone who would let her in to do what she wanted. That college was environmental engineering, and she fell in love with it immediately.

Dr. Fanara's **Why** was sparked in fourth grade when she learned about the Love Canal in her hometown of Buffalo, New York. Love Canal is an area where people built houses and schools along the canal without knowing that industries were dumping hazardous waste into it, which caused high rates of birth defects and cancer. When she learned about this tragedy, Dr. Fanara began to understand how everything in this world is connected. She says, "This is when I first saw the connection between our actions and the environment, and then, how those actions come back to affect our health. A few years later, I learned that unsafe drinking water is the leading killer among children worldwide. That fact lit a fire. I wanted to help; *I needed to.*" I've personally witnessed Dr. Fanara work tirelessly for this, forgoing sleep and payment to make change in this world. And that, my space-pun-loving friends, is the definition of a Why: when you'd fully lean in and do something whether you're paid for it or not.

Level Definition & Objective

LEVEL 1: COCKTAIL NAPKIN

Your idea, the inspiration, the aha moment, the dream you want to achieve.

Getting clear on your idea and your Why.

My Level 1

My aha moment, my spark, my idea, came from watching the movie *October Sky* at ten years old and knowing I wanted to design spaceships for NASA. Level 1 is your inspiration moment, possibly a Eureka, as some call it. It is the feeling of "I need to pursue this, this seems exciting, promising, it makes me feel alive!" Or it can be more like, "Hmmm, this might be a good next step to figuring things out." You'll have many of these throughout life. I had that one at ten years old and then another at twenty-six while at NASA that made me leave the "best place to work in America."[10]

Level 1 is "**Cocktail Napkin.**" It is concept inception. Before the birth of the universe there was...well, actually we don't know, yet. But let's say that a cosmic sperm was swimming around and found itself a cosmic egg. They meet and boom, or bang, big bang, and the universe exists. Level 1 is the time period of the swimming sperm to the meeting of the egg. (I told you this was the birds and bees of space concepts.) This process may very well start in a bar (just like the journey to inception of some humans...), which is why it's called Cocktail Napkin. Ideas that come out of taking a break from work, destressing, and then "Oh crap, I need something to write this idea down!" as the intoxicated genius reaches for a cocktail napkin and asks the bartender for a pen.

Genuinely curious myself, I wondered where the Cocktail Napkin ideas got their start. I learned that the cocktail napkin originated in ancient China to hold teacups during the Tang Dynasty of 618–907 CE. Unfortunately, it seems we do not know which idea was first sparked on a cocktail napkin. It definitely wasn't the cocktail napkin because that would be a circular reference (for all my programming nerds out there). However, we do have records of some of the biggest ideas that originated literally on a cocktail napkin. Some of these may surprise you. Heck, all of these will surprise you:

Pixar's Big Four: Four of the studio's most successful films started on napkins around the lunch table.[11] We can thank the little soft paper squares for *A Bug's Life*, *Monsters, Inc.*, *Finding Nemo*, and *WALL-E*.

The Super Bowl Trophy: Yup, the coveted reward of American football champions came from a lunch meeting between the NFL commissioner at the time, Pete Rozelle, and the head of Tiffany & Co. design, Oscar Reidner. Reidner sketched out an idea for the trophy on a napkin; Rozelle fell in love and hired Tiffany & Co. to create the trophy.

Duunnn dunnn...duuuunnnn duun...duuunnnnnnnnn dun dun dun dun dun dun dun dun dun dun dunnnnnnnnnnn dunnnn...: The theme to *Jaws*, but not actually *Jaws*, was born on the cocktail napkin. Potentially the next most famous shark entertainment to *Jaws* is *Shark Week* on Discovery Channel, which also has a cocktail napkin inception. The story goes that a couple of executives and a few beers were mixed together, sparking offhand remarks that launched the longest-running cable TV programming event in history.

Ziggy Stardust: I'd be exiled if I didn't talk about this next one. We've already mentioned him in the Disruptors, and he serves as a huge inspiration in the space world with his music. His name is David Bowie, but his alter ego is Ziggy Stardust. And it's that very alter ego that was born on a cocktail napkin in the 1970s, according to his girlfriend at the time.

Magnetic Resonance Imaging: Okay, last one, to highlight some true genius in the intellectual sense. Seriously, a Nobel Prize came from this one. It's the MRI machine, or magnetic resonance imaging. Physicist Paul C. Lauterbur's brain took over between bites of a hamburger at a suburban Pittsburgh dinner. This initial scribble led him to win the Nobel Prize in 2003.

Level 1 is your first step. You need an idea, an inspiration, a spark, an aha moment to initiate the journey. It could be as large as "I'm going to invent time travel" or as simple as "I want to improve." This doesn't only happen once. It can happen over and over again in your life as you think about your dreams. I'm the perfect example of that. Level 1 at ten years old was, "I want to be a NASA Rocket Scientist." Level 1 at age twenty-six was, "I want to work for myself talking about space." Level 1 in my thirties was, "I want to write a book about the NASA Design Levels to help people." I'll have another one soon too. It's okay if you haven't had a defining moment that causes you to fully come alive and forgo food and sleep to make your goal happen (not that that's healthy anyway). Part of your process may be to find that fuel. Your Level 1 is just that: "I want to find my fuel."

Psyche Mission's Level 1

What does the mission intend to accomplish?

Grassroots idea from Principal Investigator L. T. Elkins-Tanton. *Is there a compelling* Discovery *mission to visit the interior of a body for the first time, by sending a mission to an iron metal asteroid?*

Sylvester Stallone's Level 1

Sylvester Stallone is arguably most famous for his role as Rocky Balboa in the *Rocky* saga, although my dad would say it's Rambo in the *Rambo* series. My dad was the first person to turn me on to Stallone with *Rambo* and *Rocky*. The grit, the hardships, the insanely extreme situations that his characters go through in his movies is inspirational, motivational, unreal. But if we dive into his actual life, his personal life before *Rocky* and *Rambo*, we see that his hardships were much worse than being pummeled by Apollo Creed, Mr. T, Ivan Drago, or a sh*t local cop when he just wanted something to eat. Okay, maybe not that physically crazy, but the rejection and heartache he endured in order to actually launch himself into the career of his dreams is remarkable.

In 1969, after three years of college, Stallone dropped out of the University of Miami, where he was enrolled as a drama major, to pursue acting by moving to New York City. Many people believed he would fail because he was born with a partially paralyzed face and spoke with slurred speech. He was rejected at audition after audition. For about six years his life was an utter mess. He was evicted and slept at the bus terminal. He worked as a theater usher, lion-cage cleaner, and even starred in a softcore porn film for a measly $200. His attitude for his dream was relentlessly optimistic. Finally, he did land a role as a lead in *The Lords of Flatbush,* and with that money he decided to head to Hollywood and try his luck there.

Stallone again began to make the rounds of studios and casting agents, managing to get a few small roles in television and movies. He continued to pursue writing, and he was still struggling to make ends meet. I mean really, really struggling. This next part really hits my heart: Stallone was so broke and hungry that he sold his dog Butkus for $50 in front of a 7-Eleven so he could get some food to eat. Damn...I can't imagine being that desperate. No way can I envision a scenario where I'd part with my pup Titan for anything. Stallone literally hit rock bottom there. "I was at the end—the very end of my rope," he said.

Then, in 1975, he had a defining moment. He watched the Muhammad Ali vs. Chuck Wepner fight and was immediately inspired. He saw boxing heavyweight champion Ali get knocked down by underdog Wepner.

He had his Level 1, his Cocktail Napkin.

Steven Spielberg and the Design Levels

You might have received a Level 1 experience early on in life, but it might not hit home until later. That's exactly what happened to Steven Spielberg, the most commercially successful director of all time. (Something he and I have in common is that we are both

Eagle Scouts.) A few of his movies that are my favorites: *Jaws, E.T., Close Encounters of the Third Kind, Indiana Jones, Hook, Jurassic Park, Saving Private Ryan, Catch Me If You Can,* and *Ready Player One.* Send me on a mission to Mars with only Spielberg movies to watch for the multiple-month transit time, and I'm game!

Spielberg has told the story of how a line in a movie he saw when he was younger gave him the confidence to embrace his defining moment, drop out of college, and pursue directing.[12] The year was 1954 and Disney's *Davy Crockett: King of the Wild Frontier* was playing in movie theaters. Spielberg's parents set a rule that he couldn't see any films that were violent or sensational. Having decided that Davy Crockett was neither, he walked twelve blocks from his parents' house to the theater to see the film.

Sitting in a movie theater by himself in Haddonfield, New Jersey, Spielberg loved the film. More importantly, he had a defining moment. At eight years old he was struck by Crockett's line, "Be sure you're right, then go ahead." A decade later, he leaned into that line and put Davy Crockett's advice to use.

Spielberg was studying English as a junior at Cal State Long Beach. When he wasn't attending to his studies, he could always be found hanging around the Universal Studios lot. Spielberg was there so much that he even found an empty room where he set up an "office" for himself. He would watch as technicians edited movies, mixed sound, and corrected color. Spielberg was a sponge, absorbing all the information he could. He started making movies on his own. An editor friend of his managed to get one of his films, called *Amblin,* in front of the head of Universal Television at the time, Sid Sheinberg. "Not long after," Spielberg recalled, "I got a phone call from his secretary: 'Mr. Sheinberg has seen your film and would like to meet with you.' It was the golden opportunity...." His aha Why moment was about to become concrete.

On the fourteenth floor of the studio executives building, a building previously off-limits to him, Spielberg met with Sid's secretary, who instructed him to wait until Mr. Sheinberg was out of a meeting. Spielberg sat there for fifteen minutes, totally terrified. He describes Sid's office as the "throne room of King Arthur," with a view overlooking the 455 acres of the studio grounds, or what he called the "factory of dreams."

Sheinberg said he was impressed with the film and offered the twenty-one-year-old Spielberg a seven-year contract directing television. Steven paused for a second. He was thrilled and wanted to respond with "YES!" immediately. However, he knew that his father really wanted him to finish college, and accepting this offer meant he would have to drop out. Spielberg recalled, "I didn't know if I could do it. I wanted to be sure I was making the right decision, so I hesitated." There it was, Davy Crockett from a decade ago echoing in his ear. If he was sure, he could go ahead, but if he wasn't, he shouldn't proceed. What was he to do?

As Spielberg hesitated, Sheinberg said, "There are a lot of places in this industry that will abandon you the first time you fail, and you will fail, but I won't abandon you. You will always have a job here." At that instant he knew he was right, so he went ahead and accepted Sheinberg's offer. His father gave Spielberg his blessing for this, and within a week Steven had a contract, an agent, and a real office on the Universal lot. He knew he had made the right choice. And to honor his father, thirty-three years later he actually got his degree.

"Be sure you're right, then go ahead." –Davy Crockett

There you have it. Steven Spielberg dropped out of college to pursue directing because of a line he heard Davy Crockett say in a movie as a child: *"Be sure you're right, then go ahead."* Spielberg had two

Level 1 moments. The first was that he decided he wanted to get into the film industry—this one he thought of and acknowledged early. The second came when the *Davy Crockett* movie line hit his soul in college, and he changed the trajectory of his life completely, based on a decade-old experience.

LEVEL SUMMARY

LEVEL 1: COCKTAIL NAPKIN

- Your idea, the inspiration, the aha moment, the dream you want to achieve

CHAPTER SIX

Level 2:
Initial Feasibility

*I've loved the stars too fondly
to be fearful of the night.*
—GALILEO GALILEI

IT WAS THE end of the year, and a molecular biology professor was about to give the final exam to his thirty students.[13] Having the exams in hand ready to pass out, he paused and said he felt privileged to be their instructor and shared that he knew how hard they had all worked preparing for this test. "I am well aware of how much pressure you are under to keep your GPAs up. I know most of you are off to medical school or grad school next fall, and because I know you are all capable of understanding this material, I am prepared to offer an automatic 'B' to anyone who would prefer not to take the final." Numerous students were audibly relieved, jumped up, and said "thank you" as they left the room. In total, twenty-three students ended up leaving and taking the automatic 'B'. Seven students remained. The professor closed the door and took attendance. Then he handed out the final exam. There were two sentences typed on the paper: "Congratulations, you have just received an 'A' in this class. Keep believing in yourself."

Level Definition & Objective

LEVEL 2: INITIAL FEASIBILITY

Belief in yourself. It is possible to achieve what you want to achieve.

Has anything similar been done, something to compare/model to? Or has this never been done before, and you are the first?

My Level 2

One of my favorite movies, besides *October Sky*, is the *Back to the Future* trilogy, particularly the first movie because of a line at the end. "If you put your mind to it," says Marty McFly's dad, George, "you can accomplish anything." My experience has proven that is most definitely true.

At the beginning, though, I didn't have experience. I had faith in myself.

So many people literally laughed at me in middle school, high school, and even undergraduate college when I said I wanted to work for NASA. But you know what? I didn't let them get to me. My excitement was far greater than their doubting judgment. I had my WHY, I had my motivation. Their attitude also did give me a little bit of fire to prove some people wrong. That's okay as an accelerant to your fire, but it can't be the fire starter. You need to want to do it for you first. The doubter fuel is like sprinkles on an already delicious ice cream sundae.

Level 2 is **"Initial Feasibility."** How realistic is the concept? Is it viable? This is where most people stop. They think, "Oh, I can't actually do that," or "It's a great idea, but it's just not possible."

Sometimes they're stopped by other people saying, "You can't do that."

I had some of these thoughts myself. It seemed impossible for a kid from a small town in Wisconsin to grow up and become a NASA Rocket Scientist. Others definitely shared this viewpoint and didn't hide it, expressing their doubts verbally to laughing outright. Well, I'm here to break this false belief for you. It *is* possible, whatever you want to do. As long as it doesn't go against the laws of physics, you can achieve it. Heck, even if it does, I support you trying to make it happen—like faster-than-light travel, aka the FTL drive. I'd love to see that sci-fi become reality! Or you could invent a way around it, like warping space-time to travel distances in times deemed impossible by the current laws of physics. You might just need to think like you're in JPL's Left Field, where the "crazy" ideas that eventually become reality begin.

Does it go against the laws of physics? That's basically the Level 2 question. Is it feasible? Is it possible to do? At NASA the question is not "Do we think we can do it?" It's "Is there a basic law of nature that this violates?" In Left Field with the A-Team we say there are no stupid ideas, there are no stupid questions. Sometimes what we perceive as "stupid" sparks the most brilliant idea ever conceived. When you have a room full of geniuses (literally, these individuals are some of the brightest minds in the world), a spark can turn into a forest fire, in a good way. The ideas run rampant and go in all directions, building off each other, perhaps to evolve or pivot entirely.

With A-Team in Left Field one strategy we use is giving everyone a pad of sticky notes and a Sharpie. Remember that this room is wall-to-wall whiteboards. We create sections on the whiteboards where people can write down ideas and stick them into the appropriate category. Sometimes we set a timer for ten minutes with the goal of getting as many sticky notes on the whiteboards as possible. Then we will go through them and bin them accordingly: great, good, okay, needs work. One section of the whiteboard is called the "Parking Lot," where we put ideas or thoughts that we need to revisit but that don't have an immediate need for attention. This aids in not derailing or pivoting from the current activity or thought process by switching topics. Someone may have an aha moment and want to share, but we write this down and then stick it in the Parking Lot. Instead of "tabling" something, we put it in the Parking Lot.

There is a question we use *only* later on in the design process: "Does it pass the laugh test?" I say later on, because at this stage people will laugh at these ideas. They seem, *SEEM*, impossible, but really are not. This discipline resonates deep within me because many people did laugh at me when I said I wanted to work for NASA. To them, my goal did not pass the laugh test. But that's not what's important, that's not what really matters. What matters for your goals is what you feel inside. Do you believe in yourself? Do you think you can do it? Even given the tremendous odds against you, would you rather always wonder "what if?" or would you like to try?

If you at least try, you already are beyond the majority of the population. Seriously, so many people have ideas that just live in their heads, or they talk a big talk. Do they believe in themselves, or are they just spewing nonsense to feel good or appear better than others? When we were in preschool and the teacher asked us what we wanted to be when we grew up, there was nothing off-limits. I of course said astronaut, no joke (I'm not there yet but working on it). Others said firefighter, NBA or NFL players, a king who gets fed grapes, the ruler of the galaxy. And no one laughed. The other kids and the teacher were excited; it was a joyous sharing of dreams. *That* is what you need to embody now at Level 2, not fear of rejection or ridicule about your dreams. You don't have to share them publicly if you don't want to, but you do have to fully accept that others may—no, they will—not believe you and may laugh at you. So say your dream to yourself with confidence, with assertiveness.

Believe in yourself and in your idea. Do not be a part of the majority and stop here by telling yourself you can't do it. Many people are excited about their idea but don't solidify it. They call it a dream in the literal sense, a figment of their imagination, a "wouldn't it be nice if…" kind of thought. Here is your biggest obstacle, bigger than anything else you will face in this world: you.

You are your own worst critic, and you have complete power to kill your ideas before they even fully form. You need to go all in on yourself. Invest in yourself. Literally invest. People don't bat an eye when someone takes out tens if not hundreds of thousands of dollars in loans to go to college. Why can't you invest monetarily in yourself outside of a structured university environment? Why is it taboo to believe in yourself, to go into debt not for a four-year education but to launch a business or develop a product? We will take out $100,000 or maybe even more for our education and then pay it back over our lifetime. What about investing in yourself post-college, or instead of college, to really grow and build something?

Psyche Mission's Level 2

Is the science worth doing? Will the science objectives be achieved?

An A-Team study was conducted to focus on the science feasibility, resulting in refined science questions and potential architectures, and it was deemed financially viable within the cost cap by using the Dawn mission as an analogy.

Note: Dawn was a successful NASA mission that launched in 2007 and visited the dwarf planet Ceres in the asteroid belt until its mission end in 2018.

Sylvester Stallone's Level 2

We know that Sylvester Stallone believes in himself. That is evident from his dropping out of college to pursue acting, living in poverty for six years waiting for his big break, and even more so from his decision to sell his dog. Stallone also knew he could write. In 1974, when he was cast as one of the leads in *The Lords of Flatbush*, he also received his first writing credit for additional dialogue on the film. Armed with his belief and evidence, after watching the Ali vs. Wepner fight, Stallone spent three days writing the script for *Rocky*.

"I knew that it was going to be very flawed, but if I can get from the beginning to the end with some semblance of a character, then I'll repair the rest along the way," Stallone said.

Then he sought out to sell it to a studio.

Jay-Z and the Design Levels

You need to turn your idea into a belief. You need to turn any self-doubt into confidence or at least belief in yourself as a first step. Say it in the mirror, say it out loud, repeat it to yourself so that it's so ingrained, so that it becomes a part of you. The dream, the belief, needs to run in your blood—that it's going to happen. And that is exactly what was running through a young Jay-Z's veins.

Jay-Z aspired to be a rapper, a hip-hop performer, but he came from one of the lowest places. Born Shawn Carter in a rough Brooklyn neighborhood in 1969, he was raised by a single mother and three older siblings. Shawn fell into a life of crime, dropping out of high school to sell crack. He got shot a few times and even shot his brother in the shoulder during an argument. However, the dream was alive within him. He competed in and won freestyle competitions and eventually got a feature on MTV, when he collaborated with another rapper on "The Originators."

He thought MTV was his launching pad to be signed to a record label. But none of the major record labels would sign him. They all said no, shooting his dream down—or at least putting up a Road Closed sign. So Jay-Z found himself a detour. He *made* a detour. He created his own label, Roc-A-Fella, and produced his own music and artists. He grew Roc-A-Fella so large that he sold it to Def Jam Records and then became the president and CEO of the merged label. Today Jay-Z is worth over half a billion dollars, is one of TIME's ranked Most Influential People in the World, and is married to Beyoncé. Rags to riches to a T!

Jay-Z believed in himself. He knew that he could become a music powerhouse. Even when all the major record labels turned him down, rather than feeling down and going back to a life of crime, he doubled down on his belief in himself and took control of his destiny. He was unshaken in his belief. No amount of vibration would make his dream come apart. Jay-Z said, in effect, "I'm going to do this whether the world wants me to or not." He marched forward regardless of what others thought, including some of the most powerful and influential people and companies in his industry.

Jay-Z is a true example of Viktor Frankl's belief that attitude is the foundation of life.

LEVELS SUMMARY

LEVEL 1: COCKTAIL NAPKIN

- Your idea, the inspiration, the aha moment, the dream you want to achieve

LEVEL 2: INITIAL FEASIBILITY

- Belief in yourself. It is possible to achieve what you want to achieve.

CHAPTER SEVEN

Level 3: Trade Space

*Exploration is a wonderful way to open
our eyes to the world, and to truly see
that impossible is just a word.*
–RICHARD BRANSON

ONCE THERE WAS a little village where a blind man lived.[14] He always carried with him a lighted lamp when he went out at night, even though he couldn't have been bothered by the darkness. One evening the blind man encountered a young group of travelers returning from supper. One of them noticed he was blind yet had a lighted lamp in his hand. They began making remarks about him and mocking him. Finally, one of them asked, "Hey, man! Why do you have a lantern if you're blind?" "Yes," the blind man admitted, "I am blind and have no vision. And this lamp may not be of any use to me. But bright light being carried by me is for people like you who can see. At night the streets are dark, and you may not see the way. You may even not see the blind man coming and bump into me. That is why I am carrying this lantern."

Be open-minded. There may be more ways to approach your dream than you think. Some of the options ahead may not seem straightforward, but we should consider things from a different perspective, especially if we're dream chasing.

Level Definition & Objective

LEVEL 3: TRADE SPACE

What options are there to make your dream a reality?

What options exist? If there is something/someone similar, how was it done or what did they do? Model off of them. If not, figure out what is the closest and take tidbits from multiple things/people to combine and create your own path.

My Level 3

What are the different ways you may be able to approach your dream?

When my graduate school application was rejected by Georgia Tech, I had to open the Trade Space to determine how to continue pursuing my dream. I knew my next step was to graduate from Georgia Tech—even though they hadn't accepted me. I decided to apply to two other grad schools with the intent to get accepted at one of them and then transfer to Georgia Tech. I thought I'd have a better opportunity to get accepted as a transfer if I were already enrolled in another grad school. I had to explore what other paths I could take and not give up or stand still.

I did more than look at other grad schools. I went back to the door that had been closed in my face and knocked again. I got into a conversation with the Dean of Admissions about my application, its weak spots, and whether I could apply already for the following semester. In the end, this approach worked for me, and I was accepted to Georgia Tech.

Now that you've made it past Level 2, **Level 3** is "**Trade Space.**" This is where you explore what options you have to make your idea, your goal, happen. Everyone's journey is unique. Not all the NASA Rocket Scientists took the same path to get there. What paths are available to you? You don't have any paths available? No problem, what paths can you *make*, like Jay-Z? Like NASA spaceships going places never explored, if you're doing something that's never been done before, you have to pave your own way.

When I hear "no," I hear "not this way, maybe not right now." It means this specific point in the Trade Space is not accessible at that moment, but new areas of the Trade Space have opened up. Each action, each move, whether that be a win or rejection, modifies the Trade Space. An action may refine your options and make them clearer, or it may enlarge and show you additional options that weren't originally there. We'll see the Trade Space modifications happening as we repeat this process, revisiting the Levels over and over again on our trajectory to the stars.

If you're in Pasadena and need to get to Santa Monica beach, you can take the 110 to the 10, or the 210 to the 2 to the 110 to the 10, or the 210 to the 405 to the 10, or the 134 to the 2 to the 110 to the 10, or maybe even the 134 to the 101 to the 405 to the 10. Have I lost you yet? I lived in Los Angeles for over seven years and can speak freeways fluently. What I'm getting at here is that there are multiple ways to get somewhere. There are easier, more straightforward routes and more zigzaggy routes (depending on traffic...yuck). If one route is blocked, there's another. Same thing in life; there are always multiple ways to do something. Some are preferred or more efficient than others, of course. But in exploring how to achieve our dreams, we need to look at the different paths we can take to make them come true.

The Trade Space is an imaginary area that consists of all the possible options one can consider. In math, science, and engineering design, it can be visualized using a graph or plot. The easiest way to think of this is like a Venn diagram that gives you the options you want with overlapping interests. See the Ikigai Venn diagram example below. All of the circles are considered the Trade Space; they are all the options for you. However, the center, Ikigai, is the desired area of the Trade Space you want to dive into.

15

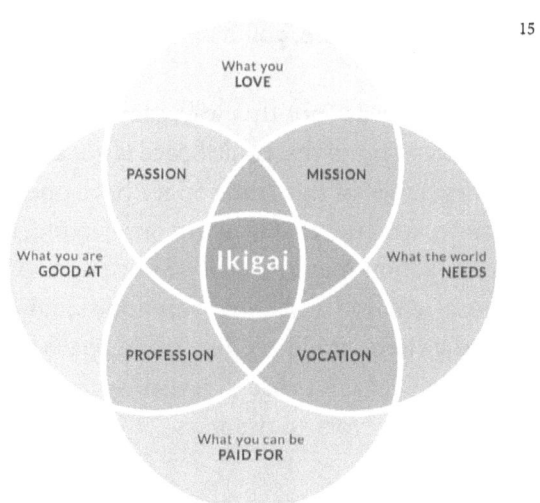

What we want to do here is identify all the possible options to progress forward. One method is to model someone else's route. We see someone else who has done or is doing what we want to, and we figure out how they did it. Then we can model that process ourselves to walk the same path, but in our own shoes. Sometimes multiple people have already done things similar to what you want, so you can explore many different variations of the paths traveled to reach success. A roadmap to success would be great; just follow the directions!

But sometimes, you might be one of the first, if not the very first, to try to do something. Here you have to create your own path. You can take aspects of others' paths and piece them together with some of your own duct tape to build a map never navigated before. You might have to create that map along the way, like the early explorers of planet Earth.

Psyche Mission's Level 3

Explore multiple architectures for achieving objectives; evaluate science value, mission cost, mission risk for each architecture.

Various mission design analyses were conducted with different propulsion (chemical and solar electric) and launch vehicle options. Then a second A-Team study was conducted focusing on the payload and instrument options. The results were four potential architectures, the identification of potential instrument partnerships and contributors, and minimum to maximum mission cost ranges.

Sylvester Stallone's Level 3

Stallone needed to find a way to sell his *Rocky* script. What were the different ways he could get this script in front of people? That's the initial Trade Space: What options are there to pursue this dream? One approach he used was taking advantage of other opportunities. Stallone was on a casting call for an acting role when he quickly realized that he wasn't right for the part. He switched gears and told the producers about the story he was writing. They told him to bring it by later. According to SylvestStallone.com, several producers wanted to buy the screenplay, but they wanted to cast a name star in the main role, rather than Stallone himself. The resultant Trade Space for Stallone seemed to be made of two options at this time: (1) sell the script without him as the star, or (2) hold out for the star role in hopes someone agreed with his belief in himself.

The Wright Brothers and the Design Levels

Wilbur and Orville Wright were trying to achieve something that had never been done before: heavier-than-air flight by humans. To do this they needed to establish a Trade Space, understanding all the options that exist that could potentially make such flight work. They were always making mechanical inventions themselves, but when they read of the death of Otto Lilienthal, a German aviator whose glider crashed, they decided to get into flying machines. They followed Lilienthal's research closely and decided to do their own experiments with flight.

They looked at Lilienthal's designs and tried to understand what failed him, causing him to crash. They also read everything they could find on aviation and aeronautics. WrightBrothers.org describes the process of invention as follows: "It's not a predictable process; you never march a straight path to your goal. Instead, you crisscross the same ground over and over again as you search for the answer that you're sure is there somewhere."[16] And that is the Trade Space: the ground you are crisscrossing searching for the answer. The Wright brothers were looking at all the resources available to them, coming up with ideas, trying to see what could be done. All of this information, from the resources to their ideas, built up their Trade Space.

From 1900 to 1903, the Wright brothers built seven flying machines in their quest for success. Each one was a test bed for their untried theories and assumptions. They crashed each one multiple times. They were teaching themselves how to fly, and they guessed wrong a lot. In those wrong guesses they were exploring their Trade Space. Knowing what doesn't work was pointing them to the ways that do. Each time, they learned, rebuilt, modified, included their lessons learned in a new design, and tried it again.

One of the most difficult concepts to figure out was how to control the flying machine. This took an intense effort of exploring the Trade Space. Part of it was looking at designs like those developed by Otto Lilienthal to see what didn't work. Another resource they explored was nature. They observed birds. What they saw of nature's fliers was that they angled their wings for balance and control. To emulate this, they tested the concept on a kite, and it worked well. They called it "wing warping," and they could control roll, banking an aircraft left and right.[17] That was just the start; they needed more control. Continuing to experiment, they ended up adding a moveable rudder, and that turned out to be the magic formula. On December 17, 1903, the Wrights made the first sustained, controlled, powered flights in an airplane, the Flyer 1, covering up to 852 feet and staying in the air for up to 59 seconds.

In doing something that has never been done before, the Wrights needed to set up and explore their Trade Space. What wasn't working, what could they try, what did work, what else could they experiment with? They came up with so many ideas, so many options. That is what a Trade Space does for you. You will need to survey the landscape, discover, and even invent different ways to turn your dream into reality. Lay them all out so that at the next Level you can compare them against each other and pick which one you'd like to try first.

The Wright brothers never gave up. They learned something each time because of their attitude—their strong-willed, optimistic view that flight was possible. They didn't let the naysayers define them. As Frankl said, they chose their attitude and then chose their way.

LEVELS SUMMARY

LEVEL 1: COCKTAIL NAPKIN

- Your idea, the inspiration, the aha moment, the dream you want to achieve

LEVEL 2: INITIAL FEASIBILITY

- Belief in yourself. It is possible to achieve what you want to achieve.

LEVEL 3: TRADE SPACE

- What options are there to make your dream a reality?

CHAPTER EIGHT

Level 4: Point Design

"Choice" "Chance" "Change"...You must
make a "Choice" to take a "Chance,"
or your life will never "Change."
–AUTHOR UNKNOWN

ONCE UPON A time, there was a little girl named Goldilocks. She went for a walk in the forest. Pretty soon, she came upon a house. She knocked and, when no one answered, she walked right in. Most of us know of this story. She approached a table in the kitchen with three bowls of porridge. One was too hot, one was too cold, the last one was just right. After eating she felt tired and saw three chairs. The first was too big, the second also too big, but the third was just right. Then she started feeling very sleepy and in need of a nap, so she went upstairs to the bedroom. The first bed was too hard, the second too soft, and the third...was just right.

Goldilocks had options in front of her. She evaluated them against each other and then chose which one was right for her at the time. Now it's your turn. You discovered options in the Trade Space. Now compare them against each other to choose one that is just right.

Level Definition & Objective

LEVEL 4: POINT DESIGN

What is plan A? What is the best path forward to achieve your dream?

Let's devise a plan. What's the preferred course of action?

My Level 4

I knew what I wanted to do in a general sense as I was looking into graduate school, but I did not know what it was technically called. I wanted to be at the front end of the design process, to be one of the engineers searching for answers at the top level. I finally came across Georgia Tech and its two aerospace labs: the Space Systems Design Lab, headed by Dr. Robert Braun, and the Aerospace Systems Design Lab, headed by Dr. Dimitri Mavris.

As I read the descriptions of each and their research projects, I was thrilled. They were right in line with what I wanted. I read phrases like "access to space, atmospheric entry and space systems engineering," and "turn ideas into reality," and I saw classes like spacecraft design and aircraft design. I knew right then that Georgia Tech was the place to go. Whatever it took, I was going to graduate from Georgia Tech with a master's in aerospace engineering.

Level 4 is "**Point Design**." This is your preferred design point in the Trade Space, your first choice in what path to take. You invest all your resources, your time and energy, into walking this path. I mean, plan A is always preferred to plan B, right? This is where you plan it. You create your roadmap of what you need to do to bring your idea to life, to make your dream a reality.

To accomplish Point Design, we take what came out of the Trade Space and consider all of the options against each other. We weigh different options here to determine the best one to go with. What is Plan A? What would be our preferred course of action? If everything went right, this would be the easiest, cleanest, quickest, smoothest path to realization of the concept.

At NASA JPL, this is where TeamX and TeamXc really come into play. Here is where we throw the computing power of interconnected models at the concept in a process called concurrent engineering. The experts are all together in one room with connected computers working on the design simultaneously. They engage in real-time iteration, design convos, decision points, and more to create a first cut at our Point Design in a few three-hour sessions. During these studies we (see, I'm saying "we" again, once NASA always NASA) complete rapid design, analysis, and evaluation of mission concept designs with the end result being one Point Design. Actually, sometimes we generate two or three Point Designs that all seem equally promising, and then the core concept team dives into each further over a longer period of time to determine the best one.

You have all of these options, so how do you determine which one to attach yourself to and push forward? NASA has high-power computer models, but what do you have? You have something even better: your intuition, your gut, your heart's desire. Which one "feels" best to you? Yes, I'm getting a little woo-woo here, but honestly the best decisions are the ones that feel right in your soul. Which option in that Trade Space makes your soul come alive? That's the one you should pursue.

Yeah, sure you can weigh out the options with finances, time, and likelihood of success considered as well. Let's not go completely crazy just yet—there's a time for that (like when all our options have been exhausted and we have to get a little crazy to find that idea in Left Field that'll actually bring us closer to self-actualization). But let's try some of the simpler ones first, eh? Hopefully, your path will be smooth. I know people have gotten to be NASA Rocket Scientists with a helluva lot more ease than my journey.

I could say, "I deeply hope your journey is smooth," but honestly I don't. The rough journey hardens you in a good way. You become resilient to everything life throws at you, in many different arenas. I don't wish disaster on you, obviously, but I want you to work for it. You appreciate success so much more, you know the true worth of what you've achieved. When you're handed something, you don't grasp its value as much as when you have to put in the blood, sweat, and tears for it. You may have given enough bodily fluids away to get to where you are now that you deserve a well-earned win. As long as you comprehend and appreciate the magnitude at which the "win" bestows "success" upon you, that's what is important.

All right, I may have gotten a bit off course with that rant. Time for a course-correction maneuver. This is something we do to adjust the trajectory of our spacecraft to ensure it's headed the right way. We fire some small thrusters to nudge ourselves just a bit to modify our flight path and improve our navigation to our destination. Like when WALL-E uses the fire extinguisher in space, but obviously a bit more controlled. Now this'll bring our trajectory back on track to Level 4 Point Design, where you decide which path, which trajectory, to embark on. You've had your idea; you believe that it's possible; you've explored potential ways to make it happen; and now you have to choose which road to take. Sometimes those first road trips don't pan out, but we gotta go on them anyway.

Psyche Mission's Level 4

A specific design and cost that returns the desired science has been selected within the Trade Space.

After doing architecture-level trades (the feedback loop), a TeamX concurrent engineering study was conducted for the down-selected architecture to get a first-level design of propulsion, avionics, thermal, mechanical, and power subsystems as well as estimate the overall lifecycle mission cost.

Sylvester Stallone's Level 4

Stallone insisted on playing himself in *Rocky*. Producers loved the story idea, but they wanted to cast a famous actor as the main character. They were looking at Ryan O'Neil, Burt Reynolds, and others to play Rocky Balboa. Stallone was offered around $350,000 for the script alone, and *he turned it down*. Supposedly he had about $100 to his name at that moment. "I thought, 'You know what? You've got this poverty thing down. You really don't need much to live on.' I sort of figured it out. I was in no way used to the good life. So I knew in the back of my mind that if I sell this script and it does very, very well, I'm going to jump off a building if I'm not in it. There's no doubt in my mind. I'm going to be very, very upset. So this is one of those things, when you just roll the dice and fly by the proverbial seat of your pants and you just say, 'I've got to try it. I've just got to do it. I may be totally wrong, and I'm going to take a lot of people down with me, but I just believe in it.'"

What an attitude! That is what was required for him to be successful. If he had a poor attitude, it never would have happened. Sylvester Stallone manifested the principle of quality in, quality out.

Michael Jordan and the Design Levels

Considered the greatest basketball player of all time (don't come at me with your Kobe or LeBron arguments here), Michael Jordan's first love in sports was baseball because his dad loved it so much. But he really wanted to follow Larry, his older brother, who was a basketball player. Michael tried out for the varsity basketball team in his sophomore year. He didn't make it; he was cut from varsity and put on the junior varsity team, which isn't crazy for sophomores.

Jordan's plan A was to make varsity as a sophomore. That's the track he wanted to go down. He saw the options and made his decision. He proceeded with plan A and then was forced to revisit the Trade Space and find a new way forward. That summer he practiced relentlessly and grew four inches. His junior year he made varsity, and the rest was history: six-time NBA champion and finals MVP, ten-time scoring leader, fourteen-time All-Star, and most recently the NBA MVP trophy was renamed in Jordan's honor ("Michael Jordan Trophy") in 2022.

LEVELS SUMMARY

LEVEL 1: COCKTAIL NAPKIN

- Your idea, the inspiration, the aha moment, the dream you want to achieve

LEVEL 2: INITIAL FEASIBILITY

- Belief in yourself. It is possible to achieve what you want to achieve.

LEVEL 3: TRADE SPACE

- What options are there to make your dream a reality?

LEVEL 4: POINT DESIGN

- What is plan A? What is the best path forward to achieve your dream?

CHAPTER NINE
Level 5: Baseline Concept

Vision without action is merely a dream.
Action without vision just passes the time.
Vision with action can change the world.
−JOEL A. BARKER

ONCE UPON A time in an Ethiopian village, there lived a boy who was so shy and fearful of the world around him that his family called him Miobe, "frightened one."[18] Miobe, not wanting to stay this way, decided to do something about it. He packed a bag and set off in search of courage. He slept in a field wrapped in a blanket that first night but was woken by the howling of wolves. Instead of running away, he said out loud, "I will conquer you, fear." At daybreak he was walking and happened upon a village. For a moment he thought, "I don't know these people at all. They might be unkind to a stranger." But again he said out loud, "I will conquer you, fear," and walked right into the village.

Elders of the village said unhappily, "We are finished. Our village is being threatened by a monster up on the mountain." It was said to have the head of a crocodile, the body of a hippopotamus; it was like a dragon with fire shooting from its snout, and it was as big as ten barges! Miobe silently promised himself he would not be afraid and announced, "I wish to conquer fear, and so I shall go slay the monster!"

Miobe looked up as he started up the mountain, a chill of fear running down his spine. That monster looked even bigger and fiercer than any dragon, fiercer than a whole pack of wolves or a nest of snakes. However, he took a deep breath and began to climb. As he climbed, he looked up, but now he saw the monster seemed to be growing smaller. He continued climbing, and the closer he got, the smaller the monster looked. Its eyes were less fierce, and no flames came from its snout. He then came around a bend, and the monster disappeared. Finally, he reached the summit, but nothing was there. Confused, he looked around until he heard a sound at his feet. He looked down and saw a little creature, just like a toad, with wrinkled skin and round, frightened eyes.

He headed back down. When he reached the village, the people cried, "He's safe!" and they surrounded him. Miobe held out his hand and showed them the tiny, wrinkled toad. "This is the monster," he said. An elder then looked up at the crowd and said, "Miobe has brought us the monster. Its name is fear."

Level Definition & Objective

LEVEL 5: CONCEPT BASELINE

Take action! Go for it. Apply, pitch, create.

Take action! Gain confidence, act courageously. What is a tangible step you can take today?

My Level 5

Georgia Tech had initially rejected my application to grad school, but three weeks later I fought to be accepted and also got myself a graduate research assistantship that paid for my tuition and gave me a stipend for living expenses.

Recall from Chapter 1 that next I set my sights on NASA JPL in my final semesters at Georgia Tech, where eventually I went through three rounds of interviews only to not be given the job. I was a few months from graduation here when I found out, so I graduated without a full-time job but got myself a ten-week temporary internship at JPL with a mentor I was doing research with while a student. He believed in me and found a way to give me an opportunity. I needed to prove to them I belonged. After hitting the ground running, during the second half of this brief internship I set up over thirty interviews for myself. I was just about to ask for an internship extension on my last day when I was offered a full-time position as a NASA JPL Systems Engineer. In other words, I was a real Rocket Scientist!

Level 5 is "**Baseline Concept.**" It's at this step that the spacecraft design team submits a step 1 proposal to NASA Headquarters for a competed project or completes a Mission Concept Review for an assigned project. They say, "Here's our idea, it's feasible, this is the best option we see so far, how about it?" This is where YOU take ACTION, where you try to achieve or get something. An example for me was applying to NASA internships in undergrad. If you recall, I got rejected over 150 times, which is why I didn't give up when NASA JPL didn't give me a full-time job right away. Spacecraft proposals get rejected all the time too. But rejection is not the end of the line. What you hear here is not a "no," but a "not right now, not this way." You're forced to go back and find a new path. A new path ALWAYS exists.

Up to this point our work has been solo, or limited to an internal team based on research and exploration. Level 5 is where we take external action. The Baseline Concept at Level 5 is where we first share our mission concept with the "powers that be," those who "hold the purse strings," the "higher-ups." We've done our homework. We had an idea, we figured out it was possible, we sought out different options to implement it, we picked one of those options and refined it, and now we present that: "Here's what we think is the best mission concept course of action."

The difference above with "competed projects" versus "assigned projects" is that competed projects are just that; they compete for funding against other projects. NASA has a few classes of missions that you can submit proposals to—for example, *Discovery* and *New Frontiers*. *Discovery* missions have a $450 million cost-cap per mission and *New Frontiers* missions have an $850 million cost-cap. Spacecraft and mission concept teams will develop a proposal and submit it to NASA HQ for the *Discovery* and *New Frontiers* flight programs. Some examples here are Mars InSight lander and Veritas to Venus for *Discovery*; New Horizons now past Pluto, Juno at Jupiter, and DragonFly going to Titan for *New Frontiers*.

For an assigned project, these are mostly known as *Flagship* missions. NASA will assign these missions to a certain NASA center to answer the most compelling and challenging questions about our solar system. These are the most complex missions. Examples of these are the Mars rovers Curiosity and Perseverance and Europa Clipper assigned to NASA JPL.

We're normally not assigned a mission in this life for which we get funding and opportunities handed to us. If you're reading this, then it definitely hasn't happened to you. Would be nice though, right? I actually call BS on that. Yeah, sure it'd be nice, but the growth you experience, the lessons you learn, the type of person you are forged into by going at it yourself—that is the true value of our trajectories. We may have a calling, a purpose, that we feel we assigned to ourselves, but we still have to fight, pitch, iterate, and grind to make it happen. In this process you will become bulletproof, impenetrable, unstoppable. That's not to say it's easy; it'll be harder than sending humans to the moon for the first time. It will hurt, you will get knocked down, you'll want to give up. I did many times. So did many of the Famous Launchers in this book. But I didn't, they didn't, you must not. You can break, that's okay. You just need to put yourself back together with the new knowledge and experience you have earned. The man who played Rocky figuratively and literally got knocked down so many times, but we all now know his name.

Psyche Mission's Level 5

Implementation approach has been defined including partners, contracting mode, integration and test approach, cost, and schedule.

TeamX played the red team during a mock review process, assessing the science and technical merit of the mission. Then a Psyche step I proposal was submitted to NASA Headquarters.

Sylvester Stallone's Level 5

Stallone was so determined to achieve his dreams and believed in himself so strongly that he accepted $25,000 for the script, rather than the $350,000 he had been offered, on the condition he would maintain the starring role. Good? Yeah, kinda, as long as he could actually perform. Great? YES! Stallone was given $1 million to make the movie, which was an extremely low-budget film, even in the 1970s. The team came in under budget by using family and friends in the cast, handheld cameras, and only using one take to film most of the footage. He used a few thousand dollars of that money to *buy back his dog.* A huge markup from his $50 selling price, but we know that Butkus was priceless. The best part? Butkus was in Rocky, too! And funnily enough so was the guy who bought Butkus, a man by the name of Little Jimmy who had a few speaking lines.

Today Sylvester Stallone is worth more than $400 million. Rocky received nine Oscar nominations, won three awards, and grossed north of $220 million. "This is one of those things where you just roll the dice and you fly by the proverbial seat of your pants," Stallone reminisced. Stallone is the textbook definition of Level 2, "belief in yourself," because damn…selling your dog, rejecting $350,000…dude had guts and a rock-solid confidence in his abilities as an actor. The once-struggling actor now has a star on the Hollywood Walk of Fame!

All of the Famous Launchers could be highlighted in every chapter, as I have done with Sylvester Stallone. They have all followed the process, the levels of spacecraft design, to become out of this world. To defy the odds and make their limitless dreams come true. They show it can be done. You can do it too. Level 5 might be the scariest step, telling the world, asking for acceptance. You're getting out of your comfort zone here, you're seeking external validation. But as we learned with Jay-Z, if the external validation doesn't come, then you can just create it yourself from the ground up. There is always a new direction, a new path, a course correction to adjust your trajectory and get you to your destination.

We do it with spacecraft all the time. Fire some thrusters, adjust the course, realign, and send them on. Realignment is literally something we plan for, and it's a better way to design. More control and less risk than a one-shot launch and hoping it gets to the right place. If you're feeling a bit intimidated or think this approach is intense, well, it is! You're dream chasing—no, you're dream achieving! It's hard because the process is rocket science.

Spielberg had to adjust to Cal State Long Beach when the University of Southern California (USC) turned him down (more on this story later). Jay-Z changed course when the record labels all said no. The Wright brothers crashed over and over again as they refined their flying machine design. Jordan had to adjust his course when his plan A didn't work out. And Stallone realigned himself to writing when acting auditions weren't panning out for him. There will inevitably be the need to adjust your course along the way. We'll explore that in the next chapter in detail.

Sam Walton and the Design Levels

Some people at this point, after achieving their dream, lose sight of their Why. Our next launcher stuck to his guns and kept the launch locks on his ego after creating a multibillion-dollar enterprise. Every single time he "took action," he did so with his Why in mind.

I'm talking about Sam Walton of Wal-Mart.[19] I bet you weren't expecting that name and company to land in this chapter. I have disliked the Wal-Mart corporation for years, but I didn't know its beginnings. Yes, currently the corporate structure and management do some very questionable and unethical things, but Sam Walton is no longer with the company—he passed away in 1992. I was quite young then, so I never knew Wal-Mart as Sam Walton intended it. Only after reading Simon Sinek's *Start with Why* did I develop great admiration for Sam Walton.

Both Sam Walton and I are Eagle Scouts, but Walton's story of becoming an Eagle Scout made history. When he achieved the rank of Eagle Scout he was in eighth grade, which made him the youngest person to do so in Missouri history. You have to be under the age of eighteen to achieve this rank; after eighteen you become ineligible. I pushed this to the very end, literally finishing days before my eighteenth birthday. But Sam Walton completed that mission at age thirteen. Dang, what a go-getter early on!

He graduated with a bachelor's in economics from the University of Missouri, then joined the military and rose to the rank of captain. In 1945 Sam began his entrepreneurial journey. He borrowed some money from his father-in-law to buy a Ben Franklin store. In the 1960s he partnered with his brother and expanded to a number of Ben Franklin stores. Sam felt like a winner and had a great idea to expand the company. He pitched his idea to the Ben Franklin executives.

Sam painted a picture of larger stores in rural areas. They could expand their horizons and serve the people that needed them most. His idea, his passion, was to serve the community, to serve employees, and to serve customers. He wanted to make what his stores offered more accessible at an affordable price for people who now had to drive hours to get them. However, the Ben Franklin executives didn't bite and passed on his idea. This didn't stop the youngest Eagle Scout in Missouri history.

In 1962, Walton opened the first Wal-Mart store in Arkansas. By 1967 he had opened twenty-four stores across America. The store went public in the 1970s and became a $1 billion company in the 1980s. By the time Sam Walton died in 1992, he had created a behemoth empire with around $44 billion in annual sales and around forty million people shopping in the stores each week. Talk about launching a company to orbit! Wow, bad, too cheesy. Yeah, we were due for one of those. Anyway...

Creating a company from nothing and taking it public is an incredible feat. But Walton didn't stop, because he didn't lose sight of his Why. As CEO, he was constantly iterating, refining, and making critical decision after critical decision to maintain and grow his company. The period after he achieved his dream may have been harder than when he was going through his Levels 1–5, because after success he found himself dealing with tens of billions of dollars and thousands of employees. Walton never lost his Why.

Walton's Why for founding Wal-Mart in the first place was to serve the people. In *Start with Why*, Simon Sinek writes, "More than anything else, Walton believed in people. He believed that if he looked after people, people would look after him. The more Wal-Mart could give to employees, customers and the community, the more that employees, customers and the community would give back to Wal-Mart. 'We're all working together; that's the secret,' said Walton."

Sam Walton focused on the people, not the money. He said, "I still can't believe it was news that I get my hair cut at the barbershop. Where else would I get it cut?" and "Why do I drive a pickup truck? What am I supposed to haul my dogs around in, a Rolls-Royce?" He was known for wearing his signature tweed jacket and a trucker's cap, the embodiment of the average American stereotype. Sam's attitude was consistent with his belief in what Wal-Mart should be.

Here's a question for you. If you ran a $44 billion business as the CEO, how much would you pay yourself a year? You built the company from the ground up. It's your baby. You've been with it through everything, the good times and the bad. The debt, the failures, the challenges. And now you're sitting pretty, riding this rocket among the stars. (Too soon for more cheese? Moon cheese? Okay, I'll reel it in…maybe.) Would you pay yourself 10 percent, so

$4.4 billion? Maybe that's too much. Two billion? I mean at least $1 billion right? One billion is only about 2 percent of the company's annual sales. Okay, let's say you're super nice and only take half a million dollars, just $500,000, or 0.001 percent of the annual sales salary. You would still take more than what Sam Walton ever paid himself as an annual salary.

At its peak, Sam Walton's yearly salary was never more than $350,000. That is 0.0008 percent of annual sales. The Why wasn't about the money for Sam. He was mission-driven. He constantly went back to his Level 1, his idea, his motivation, throughout the entire process. At every turn and opportunity, he stayed committed to serving people. That is what most impressed me about Sam Walton's story.

Sam Walton went through Levels 1–5 to make his dream come true. He repeated Levels 3–5 a few times to make that happen, which is standard operating procedure for everyone I've discussed in this book. What makes Sam stand out from the rest is his dedication to Level 1 throughout it all. It may have not seemed like much of a battle to wear his tweed jacket and trucker hat, but he did continually have to make the decision to reinforce to others his Why, his Level 1.

LEVELS SUMMARY

LEVEL 1: COCKTAIL NAPKIN

- Your idea, the inspiration, the aha moment, the dream you want to achieve

LEVEL 2: INITIAL FEASIBILITY

- Belief in yourself. It is possible to achieve what you want to achieve.

LEVEL 3: TRADE SPACE

- What options are there to make your dream a reality?

LEVEL 4: POINT DESIGN

- What is plan A? What is the best path forward to achieve your dream?

LEVEL 5: CONCEPT BASELINE

- Take action! Go for it. Apply, pitch, create.

CHAPTER TEN

Refine, Iterate, Never Give Up

*But failures happen. They shouldn't happen
for stupid reasons. But if they happen when
you were trying something risky, you learn.
That teaches you something. At least it
should. And you try harder next time.*
–LOUIS D. FRIEDMAN

IN THE BOOK *Art & Fear,* David Bayles and Ted Orland share a
parable of a ceramics teacher. This teacher announced on the first
day of class that he would divide the class up into two groups.
The first group would be judged on how many clay pots they
could produce in a month, a quantitative assessment. The second
group would be judged on the quality of just one pot, a qualitative
assessment. They would strive to make one perfect pot. At the end
of the month, when grading time came, something interesting
became clear. The best pots, the highest-quality ones, came from
the group being graded for quantity, not the quality group aiming
for one perfect pot. The quantity group was able to iterate, learn
from mistakes, and improve their process and design, thus creating
high-quality products. The quality group theorized instead of
taking action and learning with experience along the way, and
thus did not produce pots of high quality.

I described Steven Spielberg's story in the chapter on Level 1. Many people know the story of how the University of Southern California (USC) rejected him three times when he applied to their film school. So he went to Cal State Long Beach instead. He was rejected from USC because of his poor high school grades. He didn't have anything to show his talent and potential in the film industry and convince USC that his grades didn't matter. Their rejection didn't stop him, though.

Spielberg iterated through the Levels perfectly to achieve his dream by never giving up. He believed it was possible (Level 2). He figured out different ways to achieve it (Level 3). He decided on USC (Level 4), then pitched himself there, but got rejected (Level 5). He then went back to the drawing board (Level 3) and thought of another route, going to Cal State Long Beach and hanging out on the Universal Studios lot (Level 4). He went there and took action (Level 5). Then he kept working day in and day out, going through the process again and again to become the most commercially successful director of all time. USC has now given him an honorary degree and named a film-school building after him.

Steve Harvey says that sometimes you have to fail to succeed. I know we all want plan A to work out flawlessly; however, the majority of the time that is not the case. Recall that in the Concept Maturity Levels process at NASA, CML 2–4 have a feedback loop. NASA isn't just preparing to revisit Levels 2 and 3; they *intentionally* force themselves back into them to smooth out their concept. Part of the value in this is to increase the power of their storytelling. Storytelling is a large part of getting missions to move forward. NASA Centers need to convince NASA Headquarters and the U.S. Congress that American taxpayer funds should be spent this way. To do this, they need to communicate effectively. A large amount of effort goes into the storytelling part of concept design. NASA iterates on their designs, learning from mistakes, experience, revisiting assumptions, and the ability to enact hindsight.

Success does not come from reaching Level 5, one proposal, and then it's happily ever after. Repeated work to break through limitations is what makes dreams happen. I saw this firsthand when my grad school application to Georgia Tech initially was rejected, when I was rejected by NASA and JPL in my hunt for internships and a job, and when NASA put limits on my space-education efforts.

Using this feedback loop for your Levels process will strengthen your dream, to create a sturdier foundation from which to launch yourself in Level 5. This loop will allow you to revisit an earlier stage of your idea, your dream trajectory, because you will have learned more already along the way. You may be able to forecast problems that you will encounter, or you may have already encountered them. It also reminds you that you need to try, try, try and improve yourself each time. It's rare that you'll land that lucky moonshot on the first try. We actually want multiple tries to improve, harden our resolve, and forge us into iron. That allows for sustainability and staying true to your mission.

José Hernández began his life as a farmer in Mexico—but he wanted to be an astronaut.[20] At ten years old, José Hernández told his father that he wanted to be an astronaut. He was further inspired as a senior in high school after hearing that NASA had selected the first Hispanic astronaut Franklin Chang-Díaz (who is now the founder and CEO of Ad Astra Rocket Company). Hernández's father was encouraging and told him to create a roadmap to turn his dream into reality.

I heard José tell his story at NASA JPL in 2016. His perseverance along the way, and what he achieved compared to where he began, blew my mind. Not just mine: as I write this, Netflix is making a film about his life and his journey into space that is in production.

Hernández didn't learn English until he was twelve years old, as he was one of four children of a Mexican migrant family that traveled back and forth from Mexico to California to work on farms year-round. This meant he bounced around school districts and was never in one place for a very long time. It's quite tough on a kid to be working on a farm, going to school, and having those schools change regularly. But he graduated high school and went on to get a degree in electrical engineering from University of the Pacific in Stockton. Later he went on to study at the University of California, Santa Barbara, on a scholarship. After college he got a job at Lawrence Livermore National Laboratory. There he worked on radar imaging, X-ray film imaging, and medical physics including mammography.

Sounds like a pretty good track so far for him, right? Hernández then joined NASA's Johnson Space Center in Houston, working in the Materials & Processes Branch. Hernández still wanted to be an astronaut, so he applied. He was rejected. He tried again. And got rejected. This happened over and over again. NASA rejected him eleven times, before selecting him to be an astronaut on his twelfth application. *Rejected eleven times!* How many of us give up after something doesn't work out once? Even fewer of us try again and get rejected a second time. Barely any survive this point to go on to a third rejection. But to stand back up eleven times? That's perseverance!

NASA Astronaut José Hernández spent two weeks in space aboard the International Space Station, circling the globe 217 times. His original roadmap may have had that as the end goal, but I guarantee it did not include eleven dead ends. Hernández had to explore the

Trade Space to figure out how to continue chasing his dream to go to space. He needed to create detour after detour in order to keep going. He never stopped. He walked each new path he created until he finally arrived at his destination: space.

The Trade Space for José Hernández consisted of education, companies, and numerous applications. He knew he needed to get schooling in the STEM arena. He didn't work for NASA right away, but at another organization to get experience. That's an option for potential astronauts; they don't have to currently be working at NASA to apply. And then application after application. Each time he got rejected was an opportunity to find a new way forward. How could he improve his chances next time? How could he set himself apart? It took a while, but Hernández eventually figured that out on the twelfth time.

"In that process, I learned that I needed to better prepare myself," Hernández said.[21] "I started to look at the skills that the selected astronauts had and that I didn't. I realized that despite having the same education, they had things I didn't have." Each time he applied he made sure to get additional qualifications that he saw current astronauts having. He learned that all astronauts were pilots, so he learned to fly. Rejected again, he learned that all astronauts were also divers, so he got SCUBA certified. His strategy and determination paid off in 2004 when he was selected by NASA to be an astronaut candidate and on August 28, 2009, when he flew space shuttle *Discovery* into outer space.

Confucius says, "Our greatest glory is not in never failing, but in rising every time we fall." It may seem almost like you have to have plan A fail to be wildly successful (Jordan, Hernández, Spielberg, and many more followed this path). Don't let failures get you down. They are what ultimately allows you to flourish. You learn. You never lose. You either win or you learn. And we all could do with some more learning. Take those "not wins" and extract the golden nuggets of knowledge about how to improve. How can you tweak, adjust, alter, pivot, and make more progress next time? That is the mentality you need on your trajectory.

But you still gotta attack Plan A with all your might, no half-@$$ing it. Go all in, leave nothing on the table. Give it all you got. That's the *only* way that you'll know if plan A would have worked or not. Prepare and move forward with the expectation that plan A will work out tremendously, but also be prepared to revisit Level 3 and 4 after a fantastic learning session (rejection at Level 5) to mark out plan B...C...D...whatever it takes.

LEVELS SUMMARY

LEVEL 1: COCKTAIL NAPKIN

- Your idea, the inspiration, the aha moment, the dream you want to achieve

LEVEL 2: INITIAL FEASIBILITY

- Belief in yourself. It is possible to achieve what you want to achieve.

LEVEL 3: TRADE SPACE

- What options are there to make your dream a reality?

LEVEL 4: POINT DESIGN

- What is plan A? What is the best path forward to achieve your dream?

LEVEL 5: CONCEPT BASELINE

- Take action! Go for it. Apply, pitch, create.

REFINE, ITERATE, NEVER GIVE UP

Part 1—The Proof

Part 2—The Process

Part 3—The Practices

PHOENIX MENTALITY

How DO YOU launch yourself and ensure you can handle all the chaos, like the loads of lift-off, the vibrations of flight, the max dynamic pressure experienced at altitude, so that you can achieve your mission? These are *The Practices*, the tips and tricks along the way that you'll need in order to develop a **Phoenix Mentality**.

What's a Phoenix Mentality? The phoenix is a mythical bird, not of immortality, but of perpetual mortality. Every time it is struck down, it is reborn from the ashes stronger than before. That is what we are aiming to create within you. It is inevitable that you will be struck down, and every time you are, you will pull yourself back together, pick up the pieces, and reform yourself to an improved design. The strike-downs are our life's most intense lessons. They can be anything from a common "no" when you pitch something to a complete life crisis of some sort of loss—the sorts of things I experienced in 2021 and described in the beginning of the book. You know, the income loss, divorce, motorcycle accident, loneliness, death of both grandparents, all things that devastated me at the time but have forged me into a stronger being.

I believe in the Phoenix Mentality so much that I have a tattoo of a phoenix on my right inner forearm. I have had this phoenix design since I was eighteen and knew I wanted to get it tatted at some point in my life. I can definitively say that now is that time. I'm only here today because I embraced the Phoenix Mentality and built The Practices into my life before the catastrophic events of 2021.

If you put The Practices into your life, you'll be able to make it through so much more adversity before you feel you have been struck down. And when you are, The Practices will allow you to survive and even thrive during the time when you're going up in flames and turning to ash. The Practices will foster your rebirth into a stronger, better version of yourself, just like the phoenix.

The Stoics have something similar to this called the "Inner Citadel." Author Ryan Holiday describes it in *The Obstacle Is the Way* as a "fortress inside of us that no external adversity can ever break down. An important caveat is that we are not born with such a structure; it must be built and actively reinforced. During the good times, we strengthen ourselves and our bodies so that during the difficult times, we can depend on it. We protect our inner fortress so it may protect us."

I love this and want to expand on it. I believe our Inner Citadel fortress may never be destroyed, but it will definitely be weakened. We strengthen it during our good times so that it can withstand even the lowest of lows. Once we reach that low, we have to work on rebuilding it. It's still there, the foundation and general structure remains, but our defenses are weak. We've exhausted our resources protecting it, and it did its job—it did protect us. You are allowed to break, that is okay. I've broken; I've gone past my breaking point more than once. But the important part here is that even if you break, the foundation of your fortress remains. Moving past survival, we need to transition to maintenance and then growth, where we rebuild and strengthen that fortress. That is the Phoenix Mentality.

At NASA we get more and more detailed in our mission design and spacecraft design as we move through the Levels. We start with a first cut, a first-order approximation to get us in the ballpark and answer initial questions. Then it's time to drill down, get in the weeds, and figure it out down to the nuts and bolts, literally. At the end of this process, every gram is accounted for, every question answered, and every unknown addressed. We even plan for the unknown unknowns, which is exactly what The Practices is doing for you. So what are these unknown unknowns?

There are three types of information, best explained in a famous quote from former Secretary of Defense Donald Rumsfeld in 2002: "There are known knowns; there are things we know we know. We also know there are known unknowns; that is to say we know there are some things we do not know. But there are also unknown unknowns—the ones we don't know we don't know." How do you know what you don't know? You don't. In mission and spacecraft design we build in fail-safes, multiple routes to perform a function, and also put margin (or extra resources) on everything to account for those unknown unknowns. For example, we sometimes put a 25 percent margin on our total mass. If total mass right now is 1,000 kg, we'd add 250 kg for a 25 percent margin and say that our vehicle's mass is 1,250 kgs.

Engineers put margin and contingency on everything. The engineer in me forces me to quickly define the difference between "margin" and "contingency." Margin is the difference between the maximum possible value and the maximum expected value. Contingency is the difference between the current best estimate and the maximum expected value. When we are in development, we actually carry both margin and contingency on most technical resources. In simple terms, contingency is potentially expected growth, the known unknowns, and margin is extra cushion for those unknown unknowns.

We put margin on each part, on each subsystem, on the entire flight system, and then on top of everything. Our data show that no matter how refined we think our design is, those unknown unknowns creep up. We put margin and contingency on things to have enough room to absorb as the known unknowns and unknown unknowns creep in. The Practices are about building margin into your life.

By binding together all aspects of health, motivation, environment, work ethic, following up, kindness, being of service, and always learning—that is, by following The Practices—we will have a Phoenix Mentality.

Developing and integrating The Practices into your life can and will take time. You may already embrace some of these—great! Still, we need to get to work ASAP to forge you into the phoenix because we never know when a strike-down will come. We design our spacecraft to withstand micrometeoroid impacts. Those are little rocks, potentially as small as a grain of sand, traveling over 25,000 km/hr (yes metric, that's how we do it, but for you lazy Americans [mmm-hmm, calling us out!] that's 17,500 mph). A micrometeoroid impact of just a grain of sand acts like a bullet. It tears into our spacecraft, and that can happen at any given moment.

You, just like the spacecraft, need to be prepared for a potentially devastating impact that may occur at any moment, but if you're like the NASA engineers—the Rocket Scientists who designed for that—you'll be able to absorb that impact and continue on your mission. The Practices that follow will make you rad-hard. That's a term we use for spacecraft components that are tough enough to take on the radiation of space. It's a hostile environment out there, just like society on Earth, especially if you're a dream chaser. All right, let's *launch* into The Practices. I really didn't want to write that…but I did. Carry on.

The Practices

Practice 1: Mental Health & Outlets

Practice 2: Health & Fitness

Practice 3: Motivation Along the Way

Practice 4: Creating a Support Network

Practice 5: Relentless Work Ethic

Practice 6: Following Up

Practice 7: Kindness & Sincerity

Practice 8: Service to Others

Practice 9: Never Stop Learning

CHAPTER ELEVEN
Practice 1: Mental Health & Outlets

There is no normal life that is free of pain.
It's the very wrestling with our problems that
can be the impetus for our growth.
—FRED ROGERS

FIRST STOP ON this astronomical health journey is mental health. Only in the last like three to five years has it really become mainstream and acceptable to discuss mental health openly. For too long, the topic was seen as taboo or shameful. Some people still feel this way, but the winds of change are strong and have moved us in the right direction. We see a generational divide here. A majority of younger adults report feeling comfortable seeking care for mental health concerns and discussing mental health with their friends or relatives. That's terrific! But if you're not doing so already, you need to make your mental health a priority. Toss the ego aside. Men...women...other...it doesn't matter. No one is above or too good to actively work on their mental health.

What does that look like? Hmmm, maybe a mental health audit? Yes, that's one way we can do it. What does a mental health audit look like? A mental health audit is where you take stock of your current thoughts and reactions, then reflect on them to see where your strengths are and where you could have some improvement. We can observe ourselves and see how we respond and feel in certain situations. See Dare 1.1. We can do mental exploratory exercises to see how we feel about different aspects of our lives. For instance, are we happy in certain categories? Take a second to think about how you feel with regard to your home, your work, your finances, your relationships, and your thoughts about yourself. An example that I have worked through is "What is home?" I define what "home" means to me first, and then compare my current thoughts of what my home is like to what I want my home to be like. I try to do this exercise about twice a year to regauge where I am at. My therapist first introduced me to this exercise.

I believe that everyone should get a therapist. They help not only in troubled times, but also in the good times. Some of my best insights have come during therapy sessions when everything is going well. The idea that you might be in therapy has also been taboo or hush-hush in the past, especially in the Midwest where I grew up. Out on the coasts it's more common to hear someone say something like, "Oh, my therapist and I were talking about this the other day." Again, put the ego aside and go after this modality! It can take a bit of work to find the right therapist. I had sessions with three different ones before I chose the therapist I connected with best. It is definitely worth the effort here. Now, I do recognize that not all insurances cover therapy and not everyone has insurance or a lot of cash to spare. There are online affordable therapy sites like *www. betterhelp.com*. I have not used them, nor is this an endorsement for them. I mention them as an example of how, thanks to digital magic, we now can access therapy from anywhere for an affordable price. Affordable IS still a price, yes, but I implore you to invest in yourself and your mental health. The return on investment you will get from therapy will far outweigh its cost in multiple areas in your life.

DARE 1.1

Try end-of-day journaling. At the end of the day for seven days, take ten to twenty minutes and journal about your day. How did you feel in certain situations? What is weighing on your mind, your heart, right now? What needs do you have in life that aren't being met the way you would like right now? Gather the data.

In September 2022 the American Heart Association reported that 65 percent of adults say they are at least somewhat stressed and 27 percent are extremely or very stressed.[22] Increased stress seems to be a fact of modern life. If you don't manage it properly, you can become frustrated and irritable. You can even make yourself sick. Erin Michos, MD, MHS, who is the associate director of preventive cardiology at Johns Hopkins, says that "chronic, constant stress can also increase your lifetime risk of heart disease and stroke, so it is important for people to find ways to reduce and manage stress as much as possible, as soon as possible."[23]

Managing our stress gives us better control over our chaotic lives, restoring a little calm and clarity. Stress is part of our lives, it is unavoidable, but we can take actions to destress. We need outlets. Destressing goes hand in hand with mental health, and one of my personal mental health outlets is physical fitness. Not everyone uses fitness as an outlet, but everyone needs to have the pursuit of physical fitness in their lifestyle in some form (See Practice 2). Timothy J. Legg, PhD, PsyD, agrees that methods like napping, yoga, getting a massage, meditating, and deep breathing are just some ways of reducing cortisol, the human stress hormone.[24] Not alcohol, nope. No matter how many people say, "Unwind with a glass of wine," or "A beer after a hard day helps me relax," these are not healthy outlets. We're not looking for mind-altering substances to escape reality.

Dr. Andrew Huberman states that "even low-to-moderate alcohol consumption negatively impacts the brain and body in direct ways."[25] You may have heard that low-to-moderate red wine consumption is good for your health, with claims that resveratrol is healthy. But the amount of red wine one would have to consume to get levels of resveratrol that create a positive effect is absurd and comes with way too many adverse health effects. Or you may have heard the argument about gaining micronutrients from red wine. Well, those are not peer-reviewed claims or based on clinical trials. The nutrients you get depend highly on the type of grapes—the grapes, not the alcohol.

I have a bias here, as I come from a place of sobriety. I am seven-and-a-half years sober as I write this, and I have found that eliminating alcohol has had a profound positive impact on my life. I understand that for some people alcohol does hold a place in their lives. However, more and more of my friends and acquaintances who cut it out have excelled so much in every area of their life. I'm not saying that you have to cut it out, but definitely do not use it as a stress outlet. Maybe just think about a Sober 30 and see how that goes.

Experiment and find the stress-management methods that resonate best with you. Those could be different methods at different times. In an extremely stressful situation, you might take a pause to do ten seconds of deep breathing before continuing on. At the end of a workday, you might go for a jog or get in a little nap. There is not one method; consider all methods as tools in an "outlet" toolbox. Pick the right tool for the job. Sometimes you'll learn that you selected the wrong tool. That's fine; put it back and try another. Maybe knitting, walking in nature, petting a dog.

A way to significantly reduce cortisol is to spend time with a loved one, which has the added benefit of forcing you to take a break and distract yourself for a bit. The American Heart Association survey I mentioned above found that 91 percent of parents say their family is less stressed when they eat together.[26] Make the time for family meals. By the way, "family" doesn't need to be limited by blood. There is an old phrase, its origins shrouded in history, that "the blood of the covenant is thicker than the water of the womb." That is, the ties between people who have made a blood covenant (or have shed blood together in battle) are stronger than ties formed by family. In other words, "family" is what you define it to be. Your family does not have to be blood or legally recognized (I say that having two adopted siblings and a step-sister—none of us four kids share any blood relation). Families can be made from blood ties, but also social ties. Family includes the people who you love and who love you back, those who have forged ties stronger than covalent bonds. For my nonscience friends out there, covalent bonds are considered strong and unbreakable chemical bonds that bind the atoms in place. After covalent bonds are formed, it is almost impossible to break them.

DARE 1.2

Create a list of activities that would aid you in destressing. Find some that are easy to accomplish without too much effort, like going for a run, meditating, or listening to your favorite music. Then find some more involved ways for a larger reset. For example, a weekend in nature, renting a cabin in the woods away from all people, or turning your phone off for a set period of time.

Outlets are scientifically backed ways to reduce cortisol levels. Self-care, on the other hand, is an individual action that allows you to show love for yourself. To treat yourself. You deserve it. However, we are not talking about overindulgence. Self-care involves rituals to show yourself love, not to fall into one of the seven deadly sins. Now, I am guilty of eating an entire family-sized package of Double-Stuf Oreos, but that was a one-off event. I was not proud and should have stopped early. (Side note: Oreo cookies have not been to space because they are too crumbly. Crumbs in space are bad, really bad. They block the air filters.)

Self-care can come in many forms. It could be a warm bubble bath, treating yourself to a nice dinner, or watching your favorite movie and ordering takeout. Self-care is different for each person. Setting boundaries is another form of self-care. That can mean taking time for yourself, saying no to inquiries, standing up for yourself, or eliminating someone or something from your life. Queer Eye's self and culture expert Karamo Brown lists his top-five tips for self-care in a YouTube video with the channel mitu:[27]

1. Set Clear Boundaries
2. Do Not Be Afraid of the Word "No"
3. Self-Care Is Not Selfish
4. Evaluate Your Tribe
5. Don't Compare Yourself to Others

His number three, "Self-Care Is Not Selfish," is one of the hardest rules for most to grasp. You need to make sure your cup is full before you can pour from it to help others. Looking out for yourself to make sure you can do this is not selfish whatsoever.

Another aspect of self-care is to give yourself grace, to forgive yourself and not be too hard on yourself. Treat yourself like you would a loved one or best friend going through something. You wouldn't give them negative words; therefore, you should not engage in negative self-talk, either.

I have a friend who doesn't know how to do this. They get down on themselves if they miss workouts. They know they can be better, they know that the bar is higher than what they've done and they could achieve it. They say things like, "I hate myself for walking most of my run." When I replied, "That's okay, give yourself some grace," they said, "I don't do that." This is a high-achieving individual who I'm impressed by and proud of. I definitely had to lean in to understand more.

Their attitude comes from how they were parented. Their father was a tough-love guy who had an "if you're not first, you're last" mentality. "Do you think," I asked, "that if you were able to forgive yourself, give yourself some grace, you could reap some benefit from it?" Their response shocked me. They said they're not even sure what that would look like, that they can't imagine what it would be like to forgive themselves.

Everyone has an inner critic. In fact, we are our own worst critics. That inner critic can be a great use, motivating us to get things done or preventing us from doing things that would be unhealthy or from making a decision that would be unwise. However, when this inner critic goes into negative self-talk, its effect doesn't stop at those words. Negative self-talk also has an effect on our body, mind, life, and our loved ones. Speaking negatively about yourself in one aspect of your life affects other aspects of your life. Your life is not siloed; everything is connected. Research shows that the presence of negative self-talk can affect confidence and create depression across all aspects of life by increasing our stress.[28] We start to believe that perfection is actually attainable when it's not, yet fault ourselves for not being perfect. This also can lead to limited thinking and lowered ability to see and take advantage of opportunities. It's also seen in research that negative self-talk leads to additional negative habits that can then affect others.[29] Think of negative self-talk as the gateway drug to depression, lower confidence, missed opportunities, and weakened relationships.

The conversation I had with my friend made me wonder, What if grace doesn't work for everyone? I concluded that there is a fine line between tough love and grace, between holding yourself to a high standard and beating yourself up, between using pressure to motivate yourself into doing something and critical self-talk that is obstructive. I used to be in the same camp as my friend, setting an expectation of myself and being unhappy if I didn't live up to what I "should" do. I evolved into giving myself grace. I sometimes fall back into being disappointed or upset with myself a bit. But I can confidently say that embracing grace and self-forgiveness is essential and critical for sustainability and is the right direction for all.

DARE 1.3

Think of a situation where you may have been hard on yourself through negative self-talk, or a moment when you didn't live up to the expectations you set for yourself. How did you treat yourself at that moment? In this thought exercise, replace yourself with your best friend and write a letter to them, responding to them when they told you about the situation. How would you treat that friend? Treat yourself the same way.

Practice 1: Mental Health & Wellness is one of the strongest foundational blocks you'll need to implement to weather any storm. Storms of rejection, exhaustion along the journey, unseen setbacks, as well as big "T" and little "t" trauma that I detail in Practice 7. I believe that this is the most important practice, and you need to work on it early. If you are playing catch-up when faced with mental health challenges, you are at higher risk of negative outcomes. Establish a practice of mental health and wellness proactively to defend your well-being and ensure you survive the inevitable trials. Build that mental health foundation strong; it's a fundamental necessity on your journey in this life, especially if you're reading this book. You will not be able to have a Phoenix Mentality without this practice. Mental Health & Wellness is the glue that binds all the practices together.

CHAPTER TWELVE
Practice 2: Health & Fitness

The first wealth is health.
−RALPH WALDO EMERSON

ERIK KANDEL IS a Nobel Prize winner for work on memory. Torsten N. Wiesel is a Nobel Prize winner for work on neuroplasticity. Richard Axel is a Nobel Prize winner for work in molecular biology of smell. All three of them are over the age of ninety and, as of this writing, either swim, jog, play tennis, or play racquetball multiple times per week. Each of them is still extremely sharp cognitively. These intellectually strong people are obsessed with exercise, and they've claimed it's linked to their intellectual rigor over time.[30]

Health & Fitness is in most personal development books out there that I've come across, but I've noticed it's usually one of the last things in the book. It's almost an afterthought, like "Oh, and be healthy while you do all this." For me, physical health is second only to mental health, and you must be proactive about achieving and maintaining it. It's critical to springboarding yourself to break limits. (Disclaimer real quick: none of the following is medical advice; please consult your physician.)

Fitness is an integral part of my life, so much so that in grad school people often asked why I wasn't focused on personal training or something in the health-sciences field. People also asked, "How do you achieve your physical fitness with everything you have going on?" And here's the secret...the physical fitness *is what allows me* to have all of these things going on. It is how I got through grad school. It wasn't school with a side of fitness; it was fitness with a side of school. The cornerstone of fitness has allowed me to excel more efficiently in all other aspects of my life. I did get certified as a personal trainer while I was working at NASA as well, so I can call myself a NASM CPT (National Academy of Sports Medicine Certified Personal Trainer). I'm a former bodybuilder, competed on *American Ninja Warrior*, still work the *Ninja* show, and compete in obstacle-course races.

In grad school and at NASA I woke up at 4 a.m. (yup, one of those people...) to head to the gym or go for a run. This was the time that I could guarantee I had to myself before the day took over. I could list fact after fact, highlight study after study, that shows how important health (physical, mental, and emotional) is to your life. But I'm not here to throw scientific study facts at you in hopes that they hit home. If you're on the fence, don't just take my word for it. Take the examples of the legends who are out there practicing this.

- **General Stanley McChrystal**, a retired U.S. Army four-star general, wakes at 4 a.m., shaves, exercises for an hour and a half, takes a quick shower, and goes to the office.[31]
- **Mellody Hobson**, president of Ariel Investments, also rises at 4 a.m. to exercise: running, lifting weights, swimming, and cycling.
- **Jennifer Anniston**, when she's working, will get up at 4:30 a.m., meditate for twenty minutes, have a shake with matcha powder and cacao with her breakfast, then do a spin class for half an hour and yoga for forty minutes.[32]
- **Jack Dorsey**, co-founder of Twitter and Square, gets up at 5:30 a.m. to meditate and jog for six miles.

- **Oprah Winfrey** starts her morning with twenty minutes of meditation, then hits the treadmill to get her heart pumping. She swears that at least fifteen minutes of exercise improves her productivity and boosts energy levels.
- **Tory Burch**, fashion designer, businesswoman, and philanthropist, gets up at 5:45 a.m., immediately checks her work emails, and goes to get her three boys out of bed. She then fits in a forty-five-minute workout.
- **Barack Obama**, former American president, made no secret of the fact that he likes to hit the gym before running the country each day. He does both weights and cardio at 6:45 a.m.
- **Howard Schultz**, CEO of Starbucks, told *Bloomberg Businessweek* that coffee plays a major role in his morning routine, naturally. He said: "I get up at 4:30 every morning to walk my three dogs and work out."
- **Bill Gates**, entrepreneur and philanthropist, gets up and does an hour on the treadmill before starting his day.

Early morning workouts work best for me because when I get up early I can guarantee time for myself. If I tried after school or work, the day took over and other things sometimes got in the way. Exercising first thing in the morning was something I found I could do consistently and easily build a habit out of it.

The key here is not *finding* time to exercise but *making* time to exercise. Instead of saying, "I don't have enough time to exercise," try saying, "I don't make exercise and my health a priority," and see how that feels. Be brutally honest with yourself. It's hard. I get it. Especially if you have kids. I do not, so I cannot speak to that challenge, but some of those legends above have families and they make it happen. I'm not saying you have to do it in the morning, but you do have to make the time for it.

DARE 2.1

An exercise that could help here is mapping your times. Keep track of how much time you spend on social media, how much time you watch TV. Do this for a week. I want you to write out your day as it happens. You can do a bulk summary after breakfast, at lunch, after dinner. For just seven days, see what your schedule actually looks like. Gather the data. The scientist in me *loves* data, yum yum yum. Now that you have the data, do an audit of yourself and your time. Where can you *make* the time to prioritize health and exercise?

All right, that's a heavy hit into physical health. Now we're going to land on diet. (Again, this is not medical advice; consult a registered dietitian or physician.) Over the years we've been told different things like "Fat is bad," or then "Carbs are bad," or "Eat this, not that," and it can be quite confusing to know what we should eat. An easy way to determine if something is unhealthy is to ask if it is C.R.A.P.: Carbonated, Refined, Artificial, Processed. Now, don't jump up and say, "Kevin, what about sparkling water, I love it and it's water!" Yes, there are exceptions to the rule, but we're talking in generalities here. Simple rules, like eat whole foods.

Moderation is key for everything that we eat, and it always holds true that fruits and vegetables should be included in our diets. What I would recommend is a healthy dose of fruits and veggies every day with good fats and a strong protein source. I am mostly pescatarian—that is, I try to only eat fish as my meat—but I also eat chicken and turkey as well. I do not eat red meat for two reasons: (1) it's one of the biggest and easiest things an individual can do to help combat climate change, and (2) I feel lethargic and inflamed when I eat it.

Every body is different and responds differently to what it consumes; therefore, there is no one specific diet for everyone. What I ask of you here is to determine a healthy eating lifestyle that works for you. I have fruits and veggies, but I also have cookies and pizza. It's a balance of moderation across the board. I like to say try to live an 80/20 eating style. That is, 80 percent of the time choose the healthy options, and then enjoy yourself with some treats (whatever that may be for you) for the remaining 20 percent of your diet. Studies show that overeating and eating ultra-processed foods lead to poor mental clarity, energy, and mental disorders.[33, 34] Therefore it is imperative that you make an effort in this area as well.

Oh, and know that GMOs are good! Yes! According to current scientific research, there are no issues with consuming them. Ignore the marketing ploys of "non-GMO" and such. The science is clear: GMOs are fine. If anything, they are healthier now than non-GMO versions. Do you know what plant breeding was like before we learned about the targeted intervention of genetic modification? Ohhh, here we go.

Before genetic modification was invented in the mid-1980s, there was "mutant action breeding," which used gamma rays and carcinogenic chemicals to alter organisms. The gamma rays caused a random scrambling of plant genes. Researchers then selected and used those that looked like improvements. Basically, "Let's mess it up over and over again and then take one that looks like a good result." GMOs are a kinder, gentler, more controllable alternative. Did you know that most pasta comes from irradiated durum wheat? Or that most Asian pears are grown on irradiated grafts? GMOs have been an extremely useful tool in the toolkit for food and material production. Worldwide cotton insecticides are down 80 percent, and the bees, butterflies, and birds are coming back in abundance. Do you still hate GMOs? Or are you guilty of groupthink, rather than thinking for yourself?

GMOs for science!

There is no quick-fix, no magic pill, no miracle diet. That's just not real, people. I don't even like the word "diet." I like to use "eating habits" instead. Eat fruits and vegetables, don't overindulge, use portion control, implement the 80/20 rule, and find what works for you. A successful "diet" is a lifestyle change. You will need to live this lifestyle of healthy eating habits and give up the idea of on-and-off or yo-yo diets. As we learned earlier, the computer coders like to say, "Garbage in, garbage out," and that also applies to our bodies. If we fuel ourselves with poor foods, we will have poor performance. So make sure you're using the right rocket fuel for your body.

Time for another health audit. Do some tracking of everything you consume for a week. *Get that data* to understand what things actually look like. Then you have a baseline from which to make improvements.

DARE 2.2

An exercise that could help here is tracking food and beverage intake. Using an app like MyFitnessPal (free version is fine), record everything that you consume for a full seven days. Take notes at the end of each day, too, or even after each meal if you like, of how you feel. Full? Slow? Sluggish? Tired? Energized? Light? Just for seven days, see what your caloric intake actually looks like and how you feel. Gather the data. Now that you have the data, you can do an audit of your eating habits. What did you learn? Any insights into what kind of food you typically consume? Or how you feel after eating certain foods or meals?

I want to introduce you to a specific modality that can help out with self-control: cold exposure. Yup, I'm throwing you into the deep end, literally, of an ice bath. Polar Plunge! Space is cold, literally near absolute zero, so let's send you to space on Earth, kinda. Okay, really cheesy there, but the benefits of cold therapy according to science are out of this world.

"By forcing yourself to embrace the stress of cold exposure as a meaningful self-directed challenge (i.e., stressor), you exert what is called 'top-down control' over deeper brain centers that regulate reflexive states," says neuroscientist Dr. Andrew Huberman.[35] "This top-down control process involves your prefrontal cortex, an area of your brain involved in planning and suppressing impulsivity. That 'top-down' control is the basis of what people refer to when they talk about 'resilience and grit.' Importantly, it is a skill that carries over to situations outside of the deliberate cold environment, allowing you to cope better and maintain a calm, clear mind when confronted with real-world stressors. In other words, deliberate cold exposure is great training for the mind."

How do I use cold exposure? According to Huberman there is no specific recommended temperature. Look for a reaction of, "This is really cold (!), and I want to get out, but I can safely stay in." That could be 60 degrees F for some and down to 35 degrees F for others. Aim for two to four sessions a week of one to five minutes each. We see immediate rises in epinephrine and norepinephrine during the cold exposure. With dopamine we see prolonged release, meaning a lasting and sustained elevation of mood, energy, and focus. The colder the stimulus, the less time is needed to increase levels of epinephrine, norepinephrine, and dopamine.

Cold exposure can be done with an ice bath, a cold shower, or cryotherapy. Cryo is expensive and not so easily accessible, so I stick to ice baths and cold showers. To dive into this more deeply, listen to episode 66 of the *Huberman Lab* podcast, "Use of Deliberate Cold Exposure for Health and Performance."

Cold water aside, remember that the phoenix is a bird of the flame as it's reborn out of the ashes. It gets torn down and then rebuilt stronger. This is exactly what physical fitness does to your body, literally. As you perform physical exercises, you are actually breaking your body down a bit. The recovery is when you grow and get stronger. To have a Phoenix Mentality, incorporate exercise to grow stronger physically and mentally.

DARE 2.3

Take a cold shower. Too much? Start with ending your shower with fifteen to thirty seconds of the handle turned all the way cold. Then build up to more and more. Conquered that? Head to the corner store, grab forty pounds of ice, and fill up the bathtub!

CHAPTER THIRTEEN

Practice 3: Motivation Along the Way

The two most important days in your life are the day you are born and the day you find out why.
–MARK TWAIN

RORY VADEN, AUTHOR of *Take the Stairs*, said, "Success is not owned, it is rented—and that rent is due every day." I believe the same goes for motivation. Motivation is a temporary feeling. We *feel* motivated when things are good, the outlook looks good, we believe in ourselves. But damn, it won't always be like that. It'll probably not be like that more times than it is. Which is why we have to have a motivational resource toolbox.

I love Vaden's quote. I have created a derivative of it: "Motivation is not ever-present; you have to find different ways to rent it." Motivation is something we have to find and check out, like a library book, where we find what we're looking for in that moment and put it to use. But it has a return date. It's only a temporary possession. Just as the book must go back, our motivation inevitably recedes.

How do we rent motivation? Motivation can be internal or external. Internal motivation is done by thinking, using our minds to remind ourselves why we are doing something. We remember feelings of excitement or feelings of embarrassment that propel us to do something. External motivation is easier, in my opinion. There are several modalities we can access outside of ourselves to help give us an edge: caffeine, music, commitment devices, to name a few. We'll get into more of them in this chapter.

Life is hard, there is no doubt about that, which is why Practice 3 is Motivation Along the Way. We will need to continually revisit inspiration/motivation. To defy limits and break beliefs is to walk a difficult road. We can get bogged down in the weeds of our current situation and forget the bigger picture. The Why. The reason we're doing this in the first place. My inspiration for wanting to become a NASA Rocket Scientist was watching the movie *October Sky* at ten years old. Whenever the journey got tough, I had exams, I didn't do well on a project, or I wanted to give up...I rewatched this movie.

The first piece of hardware in the motivational toolbox is your Why. What is your Level 1 inspiration? Where did that idea come from? Why do you want to do whatever it is you've set out to do? Honing in on that spark is a valuable skill. The way you do that may not be as tangible as rewatching a movie like I did, or watching underdog Wepner knock down boxing heavyweight champion Ali as Sylvester Stallone did. You might have to get creative about how to revisit that moment or source.

Maybe your Why is that you want to provide a better life for your family. Put a photo of them on your desk or as the background on your phone. Add a caption if you like: "I do this for my family." Maybe your Why came when you learned that all surface runoff water is connected, which opened your eyes to a larger environmental picture. How do you turn that into something you can revisit? Perhaps by literally going to the water, the lakes or the ocean. Whatever it may be, you need to find a way to tap into that Why to revisit that spark and reignite your flames often.

DARE 3.1

Write down your Why and find a way to revisit it.
Do it now.

Caffeine can be a form of rented motivation. The consumption of caffeine induces the production of dopamine, the neurotransmitter that controls attention and motivation, which helps to enhance levels of alertness. Huberman recommends ingesting approximately 100–400 mg of caffeine in the form of coffee, tea, or whatever form you prefer. That causes a mild increase in dopamine but also increases the availability of dopamine receptors. This means that your body is more sensitive to circulating dopamine. However, monitor how much caffeine you consume. Don't overdo it and don't take caffeine too close to sleep. Huberman avoids caffeine after 2 p.m., and I try to adhere to this guideline.[36]

Another piece is music—well, audio. I'm talking about beats and speeches. Find a "pump-up" song; create a "crush it" playlist. What audio gets your blood pumping? Is there a specific beat you like, a lyric that hits home, an inspirational figure giving a speech, maybe even to dramatic music? Sometimes I work out to motivational speeches. Yes, I might be a little weird, but aren't we all? Lean into your weird!

According to Entrepreneur.com, six types of music can improve productivity.[37] Yup, seriously, it's not just for entertainment. Music can foster and grow our creativity! "The Mozart Effect" refers to research that shows that listening to classical composers "enhances one's ability to manipulate shapes and solve spatial puzzles." Classical music has also been shown to help students perform 12 percent better on exams, so crank that Beethoven!

Brain waves are oscillating electrical voltages in the brain measuring just a few millionths of a volt. There are five widely recognized brain waves: gamma, beta, alpha, theta, and delta.

Frequency band	Frequency	Brain states
Gamma (γ)	>35 Hz	Concentration
Beta (β)	12–35 Hz	Anxiety dominant, active, external attention, relaxed
Alpha (α)	8–12 Hz	Very relaxed, passive attention
Theta (θ)	4–8 Hz	Deeply relaxed, inward focused
Delta (δ)	0.5–4 Hz	Sleep

When she worked with Spotify to research the benefits of certain types of music, Dr. Emma Gray, a cognitive behavioral therapist, found that listening to music set in the 50- to 80-beat range puts the brain into an alpha state. When we are in the alpha state, we are more relaxed, open, and less critical. Some people believe that the moment of feeling inspired correlates to a higher alpha activity.

With music at 50–80 beats per minute (bpm), the brainwaves slow to 8–12 Hz, dropping us into a state of mind during which scientists say imagination, intuition, and "eureka!" moments come. What do these songs sound like? *Entrepreneur* lists a few song examples in this category: "Mirrors" by Justin Timberlake, "Chasing Pavements" by Adele, and the ironically named song (in this situation) "The Lazy Song" by Bruno Mars.

"I have walked out to race with my headphones on throughout my whole career, and listen to music until the last possible moment.[38] It helps me to relax and get into my own little world," said Michael

Phelps, the most decorated Olympian of all time. Prior to winning the gold medal in a 4x100 m relay, he put on Skrillex's remix of Nero's "Promises," and Aoki and Afrojack's "No Beef." What would you listen to in order to crush it?

DARE 3.2

Create your pump-up and/or focus playlists.

The journalist Stephen J. Dubner and economist Steven Levitt, the talents behind the book *Freakonomics*, coined the term "commitment devices" to describe reward/punishment systems that some people use for motivation. It's a way to lock yourself into doing something you may not want to do but you know is good for you. Commitment devices are things like self-punishment or gifts to yourself for doing or not doing something. If you run every day this week, you can have pizza and ice cream on Sunday. Or, if you don't get these three things done by next Wednesday, you have to do one hundred burpees or donate $500 to charity. A commitment device can be an app that restricts your access to social media apps.

Filmmaker Alice Wu successfully employed a commitment device to complete the screenplay for *The Half of It*.[39] Wu wrote a $1,000 check to the National Rifle Association of America (an organization she doesn't support) and asked a friend to mail it in if she didn't complete the screenplay in five weeks. She got it done.

What do you think serves as a more powerful source of motivation? A reward or a negative outcome? We see that loss aversion is an incredibly powerful source. Sometimes it is more powerful than our desire for a reward. The feeling of disappointment or shame is stronger than the feeling of joy and excitement. Our negative memories stand out more and can continually affect us compared to positive memories.

Research shows that loss aversion, the tendency to prefer avoiding losses rather than acquiring equivalent gains, describes why the pain of losing is psychologically twice as powerful as the pleasure of gaining.[40] This means that the pain we feel from loss can feel stronger than the pleasure from gaining the exact same thing. Basically, we'd rather not lose twenty dollars than find twenty dollars.

Michael Phelps, a household name at this point, definitely serves as a role model or idol for many. That's the next motivational tool—role models. Who do you look up to? Is there anyone out there who inspires you? Your hero can be anyone from a Michael Phelps–level celebrity to the cartoon character Hercules, Rey in *Star Wars*, or a family member or a friend. If you can't physically be present with your role models, create visual cues for them. When I was a bodybuilder, I had pictures of Arnold Schwarzenegger up in my apartment. More recently with my new passions I put nine photos on a single 8.5"x11" piece of paper hung on the wall right above my computer. Each time I went to work those nine individuals were looking over me. Cheering me on. Believing in me.

DARE 3.3

Write down who inspires you, who you look up to. Set a meeting with them in efforts to create a personal relationship with them where you can potentially receive mentorship or pick their brain to learn from them. Or print their pictures off and place them somewhere you'll see them often. Remember, though, that these are models, not copies. Be your own authentic self, always.

Where you are and who you surround yourself with can be large contributing factors to motivation. I say "can" because you are not a product of your circumstances. The story of rags to riches is one all of us are familiar with. I highlighted Jay-Z earlier in this book, showing how he went from gang banger to founding a record label and marrying Beyoncé. It is possible to overcome our surroundings, but we also can make decisions to alter our environments and surroundings, even by a little bit, to improve our motivational capability.

For example, the people around you will influence your path. "Show me your friends," says the entrepreneur Dan Peña, "and I'll show you your future." Eliminate or avoid negative people in your life. Instead choosing to be around like-minded individuals can literally skyrocket your motivation. Being in a supportive community brings out the best in each individual. Author and motivational speaker Jim Rohn says, "You are the average of the five people you spend the most time with." Maybe you need to stop hanging out with a certain person or limit your time with some family members. It's simple, not easy.

Where do you hang out or work? What places do you frequent? Not everyone can live in a beach house. I definitely wish I did, but I'm writing this book from an apartment in East Austin, Texas. Besides, that beach house might not actually motivate you. Consider the case of Dr. Tracy Fanara, aka Inspector Planet, with a PhD in Civil and Environmental Engineering, currently at the National Oceanic and Atmospheric Administration. She needs complete isolation to write. She must be away from all distractions and just focus on the task at hand. I, on the other hand, chose the bustle of East Austin because I feel creative here.

Another reason is because of the friends I have here. They are all entrepreneurs and into working out. I frequently run into them at the gym, the coffee shop, the nutrition lounge, the riverwalk, and so on. Sometimes simply seeing someone at the gym, making eye contact when we both have our headphones in, and giving each other a fist bump is enough to fire me up. I have been recognized by a like-minded individual, and that gets me going. Other times we'll talk shop or just shoot the sh*t. My creative environment right now is fueled by these collisions and the location I've chosen. Find out what situations, what environments, can propel you into motivation, and visit them often.

DARE 3.4

Do an environment and community audit. Write down a list of places and people you frequently encounter. Rank them high, medium, or low regarding how inspiring and supportive they are. What changes do you need to make?

Lastly, let's look at your Happiness Arsenal. Whoa, what is this? The Happiness Arsenal is a concept I came up with in undergrad when I was feeling like crap. It is a list of items that "make" you happy. I say "make" because in reality we choose to be happy. We have control over our emotions if we so choose. Recall Viktor Frankl's quote: "Everything can be taken from a man but one thing: the last of the human freedoms—to choose one's attitude in any given set of circumstances, to choose one's own way." The Happiness Arsenal can be as simple as a list in the notes on your phone. Write down the things that make you smile, that can help get you out of a bad mood, the things that make you feel like a kid again.

And yes, I will share my original list with you below. Whenever I was feeling down, or doubting myself, and I didn't know what to do, I would open up this file (eventually) and do something from this list, or even just read it.

My Happiness Arsenal

- October Sky & Rocket Boys
- Planes, Jets, Rockets, & Spaceships
- Knowing you worked for NASA
- Knowing your accomplishments have inspired others
- *Fresh Prince of Bel-Air* & Will Smith movies
- Penguins
- Working Out & Fitness
- Disney Movies
- Nineties Music
- Playing with Legos
- Reese's & Oreos
- A Mom that will fight for you against any odds and raised you to be an amazing person
- Adopting my little sister Elise from Guatemala
- Having a brother that will listen and give advice at the drop of a hat
- A Step-Dad that has turned into a True Father
- My loving Grandpa and Grandma Dercks (both Rest in Peace)
  - » Memories of Alabama & Up-North at the cottage
- My Grandma Carol Wydeven gives me knickknacks relating to penguins and planes
- You went to State with the Kaukauna High School Boys Soccer team in 2006
- You earned the rank of Eagle Scout on January 23, 2008

DARE 3.5

Create your Happiness Arsenal and save it somewhere you can easily access it.

There are many ways to rent your motivation. Refresh it as frequently as you need. Be proactive and not reactive. Don't wait until you feel like you're really struggling or only use it as a tool when you feel like you need it. Refresh your motivation regularly, as frequently as you can. Be proactive in maintaining a consistent level of motivation. Build it into your routine and make it a habit. The more you can do this, the less often you'll have to truly embrace the richness of the Phoenix Mentality. Implementing this practice will give you a smoother trajectory on your journey. You'll still require some course corrections every once in a while, but with a strong motivational practice, those course corrections will be smaller and less frequent.

CHAPTER FOURTEEN

Practice 4: Creating a Support Network

If you want to go fast, go alone, if you want to go far, go together.
—AFRICAN PROVERB

CHASING YOUR DREAMS can be a lonely road. Let me rephrase: chasing your dreams is a lonely road. You will need to choose to work on yourself and your dream rather than go out on Friday and Saturday nights. People will look at you like you're crazy. A lot of people will not understand. You'll forgo social events to get closer to your goals. You can keep yourself busy building a life you don't have to escape from—there is always something you can be working on. But we do need breaks; we can't always be working— see self-care in Practice 1. Because of this, you need to put extra effort into creating a support network. It's critical to have a system to lean on through your journey. Building this up will be an effort, but it will be worth it. A strong support network makes the good times better and the bad more manageable.

The "Blue Zones" are regions of the world where people tend to live longer lives, often reaching up to age ninety and even age one hundred and beyond. Five Blue Zones have been posited: Okinawa, Japan; Sardinia, Italy; Nicoya, Costa Rica; Ikaria, Greece; and

Loma Linda, California. Original research identifying these zones was done by Gianni Pes and Michel Poulain, published in 2004 by the journal *Experimental Gerontology*. And what is the source of longevity in Blue Zones? Maintaining strong relationships is one pillar of life, among others.

Dan Buettner, author of *Blue Zones*, noticed that "in the Blue Zones, people are part of a real social network and appreciate family, friends and support each other." Recent studies have shown that social support is inversely associated with mortality risk. Social integration was associated with about a 30 percent lower risk of overall mortality.[41, 42, 43]

But hold up, Kev (I think we've gotten to a Kev over Kevin basis at this point in the book, no?), didn't you just say we'd be lonely foregoing social events, nights out, and always be busy? So how are we supposed to maintain strong relationships?

Very good point, and I do get asked this a lot. The best answer is that you should forge relationships with people on a similar path as you. Not necessarily similar dreams, but similar mindsets. You need to build genuine deep connections with others who think like you. People who understand the life you live and live their own the same way. You need to cultivate the types of relationships that you can just drop into after not seeing each other for a couple of weeks, months, or years, and it's like you were together as best friends yesterday. These are strong relationships.

A strong relationship doesn't require seeing someone every day or every week, yet the connection you have is diamond-strong. You can call on each other when needed, you trust your friend's advice, you know they have your best interest at heart, and they want you to win just as bad as you want to win. CJ Finley, engineer turned entrepreneur and host of *ThriveOnLife* podcast, says that distance is never a great indicator of how well you can be connected with someone. While you may physically be in different locations, mentally you can share similar environments with other human beings. The key is to find those people who achieve the mental environment that you seek. The fact of the matter is that you both will physically go many places over your lifetimes, yet when you see each other you feel as if no time has passed because you both have made it a priority to maintain your mental environment at the same capacity.

DARE 4.1

What are the qualities of a diamond-strong relationship to you? Do you have any of these now? If not, where could you cultivate one or two or three?

What does a support network look like for you? It could include family, friends, teachers, a therapist. It's probably a combination of some or all of those. There will be people out there who doubt you, but there are also people out there who believe in you. Find them. Create that network. If people laugh at your dreams, that's okay—don't bring them along for the ride. Find those who are your cheerleaders, your fans, those who want you to fulfill your dreams. Part of this is being your own biggest fan. Yup, you need to lean into yourself, get to know yourself well. I mean really well. The kind of self you'd want to travel to Mordor with.

This support network is a two-way street. Having people in your network means that you are in theirs. It's not a take-take world; you need to give and take. You should want to lift others up too. That's how you'll know you have the right relationships. Even if they are your competition. There is *so* much opportunity out there. Yes, you are competing for the same customers, but the consumer base is the world, some eight billion people—that's a sh*t ton.

But let's say you are in direct competition with someone who, on paper, would be in your network. Are you really in competition, or can you reframe your relationship? You each have at least a slightly different perspective, you grew up differently, you experienced the world in a different way. Steve Jobs said, "You can't look at the competition and say you're going to do it better. You have to look at the competition and say you're going to do it differently." And in this sense, you'll be lifting yourself up even more.

DARE 4.2

Who is your competition? Can you become their friend? Can you help each other win and force each other to level up?

Let's talk about a few ways to find people to add to your support network, since that can be a pretty difficult thing. I mean, making friends as an adult is hard enough. Once you're out of college you can meet people at work, at the bar...maybe at the gym or just randomly? But that's not systematic or efficient. There are tools and environments out there where you can discover people like you now. We have been living in the digital age for a minute now, and we can use that to our advantage.

About half of my best friends I've actually met through social media. I was able to find people like me and connect with them via the internet. With social media you can learn a lot about someone without ever meeting them. We do need to remember that social media is a highlight reel of people's lives. I would advise looking not for people whose life you like, but for those who are in your industry or have similar goals. I found people educating the world about science or those helping people achieve their goals. You can become internet friends first with likes, comments, direct messages, and shares to learn more about each other. (When I was growing up it was advised not to meet strangers from the internet or get into a car with a stranger, but now with social media and ride-share apps, wow, the world has changed. Maybe you'll be the one to change it even more!)

MeetUp is a social media platform for hosting and organizing in-person and virtual activities, gatherings, and events for people and communities of similar interests, hobbies, and professions. (There are competitors to MeetUp as well.) This type of organization is great for gathering like-minded individuals, whether that's a group of people who like hiking, who try different coffee shops, who want to break into the entertainment industry, or who are entrepreneurs looking for support. There's a group for everything. And if you can't find a specific group that matches what you're looking for, guess what? You can create one! Then other people can search, find, and join your group.

If your dream is the entrepreneurial route, there are support groups for up-and-coming or aspirational entrepreneurs. One is called SCORE, America's largest network of volunteer expert business mentors. The organization has helped more than eleven million entrepreneurs since 1964 start or grow small businesses. SCORE is made up of more than ten thousand expert volunteers. They are committed to helping their communities thrive. Small business owners receive valuable guidance and insights, all at no cost.

There are more avenues to build your support network. You can find others with a common thread in life that has nothing to do with your dream. What are your hobbies? That's a way to find others, but it may take a little bit more sifting through the masses to get to that diamond in the rough. (If you just thought of *Aladdin* here, you get 1992 cool points because that is the year it came out. Sorry, you're old; don't worry, me too).

Let's get back on track. Hobbies, check. Fitness is a great one that can be a common thread across individuals from many different backgrounds and goals. I've met most of my adult friends through fitness of some sort, whether while working out or through events like *American Ninja Warrior*. There is immediately a commonality.

DARE 4.3

What groups can you join? Where can you find others "like" you? Make a list of things you do outside of dream chasing. How can you build communities in these areas?

You are the product of your inner circle's inner circle. Your friends' friends. It's a compounding effect because your inner circle is not the same as that of your members. So when you're creating this support network and choosing who to keep close to you in your life, you'll also need to explore who those people keep close to them. Would you be comfortable with the members of their inner circle being members of your inner circle? If not, you might want to take a pause.

What You Think Your   What It Actually
Inner Circle Looks Like   Looks Like

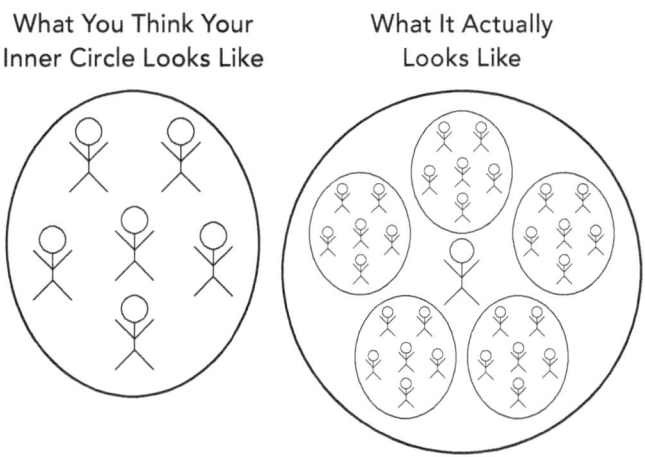

We raise or lower to the standards of our friends, just as they raise or lower ours. Let's say you enjoy Cheesecake Factory, but two or three of your inner-circle members are big into health and fitness. You won't be eating at Cheesecake Factory with them. Instead, you start eating healthier when you share meals together and frequent the factory of queso less and less. You have risen to the standard of those friends. If, on the other hand, your friends like to drink when you get together, you are six times more likely to drink.

This isn't just anecdotal. A study published in 2007 in the *New England Journal of Medicine* showed that if your friends or siblings become obese, you're actually more likely to become obese as well, even if your friends live hundreds of miles away.[44] That's kinda freaky. Harvard and University of California San Diego (UCSD) researchers mapped the data to find that "when a person becomes obese, the chances that a friend will become obese increases by 57 percent. Siblings of obese people have a 40 percent increased risk of obesity, and their spouses' risk increased by 37 percent."

Put in the work to build this leg of support, the gantry that holds you upright as a foundation, and you can blast off to break through the barriers of this world and enter the space where dreams become reality. Your Phoenix Mentality is only as strong as your relationships. You need to have a deep relationship with yourself, diamond-strong ones with others, and a community of support.

CHAPTER FIFTEEN

Practice 5:
Relentless Work Ethic

*If people knew how hard I had to work to gain my
mastery, it would not seem so wonderful at all.*
—MICHELANGELO

RECENTLY I RETURNED to Wisconsin to visit my parents. My dad
decided that we'd cut down a dead tree in the back yard. He told
me Uncle Jim was coming over in a bit and we'd make quick work
of it. While waiting for him to arrive, I brushed my teeth, shaved,
and went to the bathroom. By the time I came out of the bathroom
ten minutes later, the tree was down on the ground and Uncle Jim
was cutting it up into pieces.

My father, Mike Wydeven, is the textbook example of work ethic in
action, and so is my Uncle Jim. Witnessing his practices of getting
things done growing up instilled the same ethic in me. Even though
he may have not wanted to do things, he did them. They had to get
done. There was no "Someone else will do it," or "We'll do it later."
His consistent attitude was, "All right, let's get to work and get this out
of the way." Whether that was cutting the lawn, shoveling the snow
in the driveway, changing the oil in the car, redoing the landscaping,
washing the dishes, or going over to someone else's house to do these
exact same things, my dad's work ethic is impeccable.

Thomas Jefferson said, "I'm a believer in luck, and I find the harder I work the more I have of it." You must do the things that others won't so that you can have the things that others don't. We're not talking materialistic things here, but opportunities and choices, especially the choice in how to spend your time. Time is our most precious resource: once it's used, you can never get it back. We need to live our lives with a relentless work ethic. This requires self-discipline and willpower.

You will be making sacrifices now to enjoy later. This is a tough one. Ever hear of the marshmallow test? There seems to be some conflicting data about how this worked out, but nonetheless it conveys a great idea. The "Stanford Marshmallow Experiment" was a study in 1972 led by psychologist Walter Mischel about delayed gratification.[45] A child of four or five was given a marshmallow and told that they could eat it if they wanted. They were also told that if they did not eat that marshmallow but waited for a brief period of time, they would receive another marshmallow and get to eat both of them. Then the researcher left the room for about fifteen minutes.

In follow-up studies, those children who were able to delay gratification and wait for the second marshmallow tended to have better life outcomes, as measured by SAT scores, educational attainment, body mass index (BMI), and other life measures.

A new follow-up study published in 2020 with the involvement of Mischel disavowed some of those findings, noting that the marshmallow test itself wasn't a statistically significant predictor of futures.[46] This study did conclude that researchers could potentially glean insights about a child's future from the subject's parents and the subject's own assessments of self-control as they aged.

The great news is that you're not destined for a better or worse life by age four—you have the ability to adapt and change. Your parents and your awareness of control as you grow older are the determining factors. Delayed gratification is how we get the things that really matter in this life. Anything that's worth having requires work. We study, we work hard, we prepare, so that when it's game time we can crush it. Instant gratification sets us up for detours, distractions, and getting lost along our trajectory to our dreams. What I'm describing is a simple principle but not an easy one to live by, especially in a culture that promotes instant gratification.

How do we improve our self-control to delay gratification on this journey of ours? I'm glad you asked. Incorporating Practices 1, 2, 3, and 4 will go a long way in helping you out here.

Practice 1: Mental Health & Outlets
Practice 2: Health & Fitness
Practice 3: Motivation Along the Way
Practice 4: Creating a Support Network

There are times when I may not make my dad and uncle proud. I am not perfect, and you do not have to be. For instance, when I was an undergrad I lived in a house with seven guys. Our operating phrase was, "Why do it today when we can do it tomorrow?" and that mostly meant cleaning and organizing the house. I mean, it was eight dudes, in college—it wasn't the most well kept of college houses. We all have our moments. That's all right. I've grown up and learned from that. So can you, from your imperfections. We still have time. This is why we're going through the practices. Just as with motivation, we can be graced by constant or frequent reminders to instill these practices into our lives.

DARE 5.1

What's something you've been putting off that you should get done? Get to it sooner rather than later. What is the specific next actionable step toward that thing? It could be taking out the trash, which means you need to pull the trash bag out of the can and tie it. That's the next actionable step. If it's reaching out to someone, it's drafting up an email with their address in the "To" line. Get it done. Be like Mike and Jim Wydeven.

In 2022 we can literally have anything we want and anytime. Hungry? UberEats. Bored? Instant streaming shows and movies. Lonely? Social media (which actually makes us lonelier…). Curious about something? Google. Thirsty? Running water. Questions? Global connectivity for developed countries.

How can we even get stuff done with all these temptations of instant gratification? A lot of people are fine with that—they are content. They utilize all these resources to live a comfortable life. But that's not you. If you're reading this, you're not one of those people—or you are but you'd like to launch yourself out of that category. Even if this isn't you, I guarantee there are still areas where you can make improvements. I know I can.

To develop a relentless work ethic, eliminate distractions and make it easier to drop in to tasks related to accomplishing your dream. That's essential. It goes hand in hand with the environment audit we did earlier. Ask yourself, "How can I foster an environment that has fewer temptations that distract me from a relentless work ethic?" Yes, self-control and willpower are great assets, but you can modify your environment so you don't have to lean into them as much. We can create a smoother way to embody the work ethic of our dreams. For instance, you could make physical changes, like creating a home office or working in a specific coffee shop where you're able to be productive. You could delete distracting apps (like Instagram or Twitter) off of your phone. You could write out a set of guidelines that you'll adhere to in making this lifestyle change. Each of us has it in us to be the textbook example of work ethic. To be a Mike Wydeven, Jim Wydeven, a new YOU.

DARE 5.2

What temptations and distractions do you currently have in your life? What tangible and intangible things can you think of? Say you have a home office, but the fridge and TV are too close. Is it better to work at a coffee shop or coworking space? Or maybe you need to turn your phone on Do Not Disturb mode while you're working. Maybe you should proactively tell friends that you're taking a pause from nonessential social engagements while you work on your dream. Take stock of the things that may derail you from a relentless work ethic, and then make a change.

Establish a relentless work ethic. Never give up. Make sacrifices now to enjoy later. Make decisions and take actions that your future self will thank you for. Skip the party to study. Don't go out at night—stay in, working toward your goals. It'll be worth it. I promise. You need to do the things others won't so you can have the things others don't. Doing this will develop the Phoenix Mentality in you, not only by moving you forward, but also by avoiding those situations which can move you backward.

CHAPTER SIXTEEN
Practice 6: Following Up

The answers will be given to those
who are bold enough to ask.
−AMIT KALANTRI

NBA HALL OF Famer Moses Malone holds the record for the most offensive rebounds in NBA history with 6,731.[47] A professional basketball player from 1974 through 1995 as a center, he was named the NBA Most Valuable Player three times, was a twelve-time NBA All-Star, and was an eight-time All-NBA Team selection. Critics said that Moses Malone had concrete hands, but he would rebound his own missed shot, sometimes three or four times a possession. He was relentless at going in and getting his own rebound. He was 6'10" and 215 pounds, but still he knew that he must master the fundamentals to succeed in the game.

Too many of us try once, hope for the best, and let "destiny" decide what happens. No! We can make our own destiny. In basketball, you don't just throw up a shot and walk away, assuming it's going in. You follow it up and go in for the rebound. Only the arrogant players shoot their shot, keep their hand in the air, and like to put on a show. Maybe they even start walking backward toward the other end of the court. But the real show is when the player shoots their shot and then drives right to the hoop, preparing for a rebound opportunity to put it back up and get the points. Those are the fundamentals of basketball. That's how the truly dedicated players, those with basketball in their soul, show their ambition to win rather than play for show.

We must always follow up when pursuing our dreams. You are the only person who has your dream as the number-one priority. Even those who want you to succeed have other things on their minds, like themselves and their dreams. You are the only one who will always be looking out for yourself. This means we need to be consistent in our communication and touch points along the way, "touch points" meaning number of contact occurrences. Submitting an application is one touch point. Sending an email to check on your application is a second touch point. Having the interview, a third touch point. Sending a thank-you email after the interview, a fourth touch point. And following up after a week if you haven't heard anything, stating you're still interested and would like to continue the conversation, a fifth touch point. They say the squeaky wheel gets the oil—well, that's true. The more touch points you have, the more top-of-mind you are for that individual or organization. Now, don't go overboard here—you do need to use finesse and strategy in your touch points. Don't be a stalker or overbearing. Each touch point needs to have a purpose.

Consistent use of touch points applies to more than career/business relationships. Make sure you're following up with friends and family too. Did a friend tell you that they had a rough day last week? Check in with them. See how they are doing. Maybe a loved one is going through a divorce; check in on them. Or possibly someone just won an award; reach out to congratulate them. Continue to foster your personal relationships. This goes into our fourth practice of Creating a Support Network. (You'll see that a lot of these practices overlap and go hand in hand.) Each one of these practices can and should be applied both to your professional life and to your personal life.

The ability to implement each of these practices through all aspects of life is what is going to allow you to survive the darkness. Yes, there will be darkness, I'm not going to sugarcoat it for you. You've learned of my darkness, and it's these practices that got me through it. We've been focusing mostly on using them to skyrocket yourself when life is neutral or good, but they are just as important during the launch failures, the scrubs, the aborted missions, the catastrophes. I would like to add that these practices, and specifically Following Up, aren't just for you. They also are for the other people in your life. We'll get into this more in the next two practices, but seriously, following up with others just might be the light they need to continue on. Or it could be the power-up mushroom in Mario to make them feel superhuman.

DARE 6.1

What is an area of your life or your goal trajectory where you can increase your touch points? Set a strategy and initiate the task of increasing touch points.

You never lose; you either win or you learn. (Actually, you do lose if you don't learn.)

Let's say you don't "win" at something. Follow up and ask for feedback. Seek insight into why you didn't win and how you can modify your approach for next time. Because there is no actual failure, there is just "not this way, not right now." Take a pause and figure out how to go at it again a slightly different way. There is no failure; there is only giving up. You must keep going until you make your dream happen. Continue to iterate and pursue until you make that dream a reality.

Remember that story about how Georgia Tech initially rejected my application to grad school, but three weeks later I fought to get accepted and also got myself a graduate research assistantship, which paid for my tuition and gave me a stipend for living expenses? Here's the longer version of what happened. When I received the rejection email from Georgia Tech Admissions, I was heartbroken. I sat in my summer internship cubicle feeling as if my hopes and dreams had been smashed. But I only indulged that feeling for a few minutes. I quickly switched gears and became motivated to find out why, to figure out what my weaknesses were so that I may improve.

My desire for feedback and improvement sparked a month-long email exchange with the Associate Chair for Graduate Programs and Research, Dr. Jagoda. He informed me that he was traveling, so I decided to send two emails for each one of his emails back to me. My intent was to keep my name in his mind, show perseverance, and have my messages be at the top of his inbox. (Looking back on that, I must have been so annoying—that's a lot of emails. I've learned better touch-point strategies since then.)

Meanwhile, I wasn't just waiting around to see what would happen with Georgia Tech. I started my applications for the University of Texas-Austin and the University of Maryland because they offered programs in my secondary research interests. My backup strategy was to get accepted into one of these schools, then transfer to Georgia Tech. No matter what, I was going to accomplish my goal of graduating from Georgia Tech…by any means necessary.

What happened next I definitely did not expect. I received a call from Dr. Jagoda on Friday, July 26, 2013, while I was working on a new vane pump design for the F-16 Fighting Falcon fighter jet. That was a day after I had asked Dr. Jagoda if I could already apply for the following semester. I stated this was in an effort to make sure there would be a spot available. He told me that he had heard my passion, seen my initiative, and witnessed firsthand my dedication and perseverance about attending Georgia Tech. Dr. Jagoda said, "I've heard enough. I have created and opened up a spot for you in the aerospace program." After we hung up, I sat there for a few moments taking in what had just happened. I was speechless, in awe of what I had just accomplished. Following up works, my friends.

Asking for feedback is different than receiving unsolicited feedback. When someone chooses to share their unsolicited opinion, our defenses rise up. We tend to debate, rationalize, and reject the feedback. But when we intentionally and strategically ask for feedback, we put ourselves in a better position to hear it. We're more open to listening, asking questions for clarification, and eventually accepting the feedback. As Warren Buffet has said, "Honesty is a very expensive gift; just don't expect it from cheap people."[48]

Bill Gates said, "We all need people who will give us feedback. That's how we improve." Feedback is another tool to boost us into the orbit we desire. We can get another perspective on what we're doing. But we need to get it from the right sources. As Warren Buffet said, we can't get effective feedback from the wrong people. You must want feedback as well; you must want to improve. If you're sitting there in your own world thinking that you got it all figured out, well, you're probably not reading this book, but you need a reality check and definitely need some feedback. Reel in that ego and cast out some humility. You're a dream chaser right? You want to be a Launcher. To achieve those goals, you need to be great. NBA coach and former player Doc Rivers tells us how it is: "Average players want to be left alone. Good players want to be coached. Great players want to be told the truth." In order to reach that orbit you desire, you need to be a great player.

DARE 6.2

Find three people who genuinely have your best interests at heart and ask them for feedback. Ask them to list three strengths and three areas of improvement. Be open, ask questions, and implement change.

You might be a little afraid to hear some of what they have to say. It might be intimidating to follow up. That's normal. What we are working on here is to make you supernatural. You are Daring Mighty Things, and to do that, we need to get you out of your comfort zone. If you feel that you have this on lock, excellent! I challenge you to explore embracing feedback further and get super real with yourself.

Is there feedback that you haven't incorporated? Why? Is it just someone else's opinion and it doesn't aid you in reaching your next orbit? That could entirely be the case. Let's think about that for a second. We are following up to keep ourselves top of mind for the individuals and organizations that'll raise us up closer to our goals. We are asking for feedback from professionals, peers, and loved ones in an effort to improve ourselves. However, let's keep something in mind that I've said before: You are the only one genuinely looking out for Number One, yourself. Not everything you hear will be useful. Be open to the feedback, analyze it, and determine if those changes are right for your journey.

For example, conventional advice may not actually be appropriate for you. You'll need to be creative. Nothing in this world, this life you're living, is absolute. We are not siths; there are no absolutes (which in itself is an absolute, Obi Wan…). There isn't a definitive answer to anything. Don't blindly accept feedback, even if it's from those you admire or love. Hear it, ask questions for clarification, and see how it fits into your overall roadmap of where you want to go.

You are the expert of your Level 1, your idea, your aha moment. Only you can steer your dreamship the right way. You get to choose what fuel to fill it up with. You'll be presented with many options; some will tell you that one fuel is better than another. That is their opinion based upon their perspective with their life experiences and knowledge. It may very well be the best option for you; just take it with a grain of sodium chloride and decide if it's right for you.

Our phoenix is a being of perpetual mortality, coming back again and again. That is exactly why following up is part of the Phoenix Mentality. You will be going back again and again, over and over.

CHAPTER SEVENTEEN
Practice 7:
Kindness & Sincerity

*Spread love everywhere you go. Let no one
ever come to you without leaving happier.*
–MOTHER TERESA

SOON AFTER I moved to Los Angeles, I went shopping in a Ralphs grocery store. I was walking around with my hand basket, picking up a few things, wandering all over the store because I had no idea where things were yet. Lines of people and their carts waiting to check out began to form. I was still wandering, so I headed back to the other end of the store, walking in the space between the aisle and the checkouts, now full of people. As I approached a line to cut through I said, "Excuse me," and a lady stared at me like a deer in headlights. She said, "You're not from here, are you?" I said, "No, I just moved. Why?" She responded, "Because you are polite. Never lose that, especially in this city. It'll get you farther than anything else."

Just be kind. I really thought about this chapter containing only those three words. Big and bold, taking up the entire page, one word on each line. It's so simple and easy this time. Just be kind. In *Think Like a Monk*, Jay Shetty writes, "There is toxicity everywhere around us. In the environment, in the political atmosphere, but the origin is in people's hearts. Unless we clean the ecology of our own heart and inspire others to do the same, we will be an instrument of polluting the environment. But if we create purity in our own heart, then we can contribute great purity to the world around us." Goodness breeds goodness. Be good to others, and it will spread. Do as the Dalai Lama says: "If you can, help others; if you cannot do that, at least do not harm them."

"Please" and "thank you" are still magic words. Seriously. What we are told as kids holds true for adults. The words "please" and "thank you" show appreciation in our uncontrollably busy society. Saying them takes a fraction of a second but can make the world stop in an instant. "Please," "thank you," and I'll add "excuse me."

Why does it seem that the world lacks kindness? Has it always been like this? Is it truly the case that the world is unkind, or are we just seeing more of it with the digital age? At a top level, yes, the *world* is unkind. The saying "life isn't fair" is a saying because it's true. We cannot *expect* things; we cannot say we *deserve* things. We are not *entitled* to anything. Having an expectation or entitlement mindset produces anger, resentment, and bitterness. We must work on ourselves to avoid these thoughts.

When we work hard chasing our dreams, we may start to feel we *deserve* to win. I think this at times, for sure: "Why haven't I won yet?! I've put in so much effort, I deserve it!" Unfortunately, the reality is we don't "deserve it," and that mindset actually hinders us. In order to truly succeed, you have to do the work as if you will never succeed. Day in and day out you must perform selflessly. This goes back to your Why. You'd have to do this even if you wouldn't get paid for it. It's your Why, your passion, your love. The thing that keeps you up at night. Work tirelessly and selflessly, and the universe will bring your dream to reality.

What I'm describing is the ideal situation, the purest of heart and intentions, truly altruistic with no distractions of any sense of self. One, if not the best, example of this is Mother Teresa. She is a unicorn, an outlier, a miracle—and an actual saint. But let's face it, we all have a sense of self, and even others. The perfect situation is that we work selflessly, but that is not reality. Wanting to do the work in the first place is a form of selfishness, because we want to. And there is nothing wrong with that! I'm sure Mother Teresa got enjoyment out of helping others. Photos of her show a pretty joyous woman. But what's important here is that we strive for the ideal, an altruistic approach. As we work toward and approach the ideal, our lives do get better. We feel better about ourselves, our mental health improves, and people are more likely to help us out.

DARE 7.1

Where can you incorporate more kindness into your life? How many times are you using "please," "thank you," and "excuse me"? Try holding the door open for someone, or the elevator for someone approaching. Maybe ask, "What floor?" in the elevator. That's a small act of kindness that can go a long way. Want to kick it up a notch? Buy groceries or gas for another person.

Smile. Smiles. Smiling. You probably have heard of the theory of evolution by natural selection and survival of the fittest. But how about Charles Darwin's Facial Feedback Response Theory?[49] The facial feedback hypothesis states that our facial expressions affect our emotions. It holds that smiling can make us feel happy even when we feel sad. It is the act of smiling that produces a happy feeling, not the other way around. Also, smiling is said to be evolutionarily contagious. A smile breeds a smile, just as a yawn causes others to yawn. Try it. Smile at a stranger and see what happens.

Smiles feel good, great. But did you know smiles can also help you be more successful and live longer? A 2010 Wayne State University research project examined the baseball-card photos of Major League players in 1952.[50] The study found that the span of a player's smile could actually predict his life span. How much of a difference are we talking about here? Well, the players who didn't smile lived an average to 72.9 years old, while players with beaming smiles lived an average of 79.9 years. A UC Berkeley thirty-year longitudinal study examined yearbook student smiles of women in college to see if there was a correlation between intensity of smile and well-being and success throughout their lives.[51] The widest smilers ranked the highest in fulfillment and duration of marriage, standardized test scores of well-being and general happiness, and being an inspiration to others.

Smiles are associated with all the emotions we consider positive: happiness, joy, surprise, and trust. We see a smile and we see positivity. Think of something you like, and what happens? You smile. Maybe just on the inside, but that smile gives you an improved feeling, a little happiness. The trajectory of your dream is tough; you need to be smiling during your voyage. As Sam Walton showed, the journey isn't over once the destination is reached. This path you're on is not a means to an end; it's a life you're building that you don't need to escape. The process to do that may not always be glorious, but it should make you smile knowing what you're working toward. There will definitely be many, many times you don't want to smile. Through the rejection, the roadblocks, the obstacles, the unknowns, the uncertainty, the discomfort and fear, do your best to smile more. Think back to your Level 1 in those times, and smile.

DARE 7.2

Just smile more. And smile at strangers.

Okay, it may not be *that* easy for some of us to just be kind or smile. We are each riddled with trauma in our own ways. That could be little "t" trauma, like non-life-threatening injuries, loss of a job, emotional abuse, death of a pet, bullying or harassment, and loss of significant relationships, or big "T" Trauma, including serious injury, sexual violence, repeated abuse, death of a parent, or life-threatening experiences. These traumatic events may make us feel resentful, hateful, or aggravated in aspects of life.

We cannot let our past dictate our future. We are not a product of our circumstances, but a product of our decisions, to paraphrase Stephen Covey, the famed author of *The 7 Habits of Highly Effective People*. We get to choose our responses. We may have reactions, but there is that gap between stimulus and response, as taught by Viktor Frankl: "Between stimulus and response there is a space. In that space is our power to choose our response. In our response lies our growth and our freedom." Choose your freedom. It will take work to manage and overcome the little "t" and big "T" traumas. They are no joke. Mental and emotional health are serious things, and problems like PTSD (post-traumatic stress disorder) should be handled with caution and the supervision of a medical professional. We've touched upon mental health in several of these practices. Use the tools that are out there to dig deep and design yourself the way you see best.

Putting little and big "t" trauma aside, we're also riddled with anxiety and stress daily. They come at us through social media, billboards, other advertisements, our family, work, commuting, traffic, maybe a line at the coffee shop when we're in a rush. There is no avoiding it. Stress and anxiety are a barrier to being our best selves, holding our heads high and projecting kindness and smiles. They can weigh us down and get increasingly heavy as time goes on. Remember to give yourself grace. We're not perfect, success takes time, and there will always be mistakes and missteps in our future. Don't be too hard on yourself. We strive for the ideal but know we cannot actually live it. It can be very difficult to manage stress and anxiety, to set them aside and leave the world a better place than we found it. To rephrase the famous Maya Angelou, people may not remember what you did, but they will remember how you made them feel.

You have the ability to choose, to overcome, to change, to expel the negativity and project kindness and sincerity. Viktor Frankl taught us this, and we saw examples among our Famous Launchers. Achieving dreams is difficult, becoming an admirable person is difficult, and to do both is a miraculous feat that you can only achieve when you follow the NASA Design Levels process and implement The Practices into your life, forging your Phoenix Mentality.

CHAPTER EIGHTEEN
Practice 8:
Service to Others

The secret to living is giving.
–TONY ROBBINS

TONY ROBBINS, LIFE coach and bestselling author, has shared some very powerful stories about being of service to others.[52] A moment that changed his life occurred when he was eleven years old.

His family was poor. They had no money or food for Thanksgiving. But his family received food through a stranger, and that changed his life. He has no idea who it was, even to this day, and it wasn't the food itself that was life-changing, but the fact that strangers cared. This profound moment in his life made him then care about strangers. "It shifted the direction of my life so I know the value of that." Tony started feeding other families and eventually started a company where he got his employees involved in feeding strangers too. Between himself and his company, they feed millions of families each year.

His *giving* origin story began when he was seventeen. To save money he would ride his bike from Venice, California, to an all-you-can-eat buffet called El Torito in Marina del Rey. He was eating everything he possibly could at this restaurant on the water when a very attractive woman came in with a kid dressed in a suit and little vest. This kid was a perfect gentleman, holding the door open for his mom, pulling out her chair for her to sit down, and just staring into her eyes. Seeing this moved Tony in a way he didn't expect, as he was in the mindset of selfishness and total scarcity. But witnessing this act of love and respect changed him. After paying his $5.95 bill, Tony had about $17 left in his pocket. He walked up to the little boy, introduced himself, and congratulated him for being such a gentleman, calling him "a class act."

"Ah, she's my mom," the kid said. "It's so cool you're taking her to lunch like this," Tony replied. But the boy explained he couldn't really take her to lunch because he was only eleven years old and didn't have a job yet.

Tony was not going to let that happen. Be it the holy spirit, a rush of endorphins, a moment of bliss, something seized him. He reached in his pocket, grabbing the $17 he had left in the world and gave it to the kid, telling him yes, he was taking his mom to lunch. The kid's eyes got super big. He said he couldn't accept it. "Yes, you can because I'm bigger than you," Tony said, and he flew out of that restaurant on cloud nine, skipping. He was euphoric, even though he just gave away his last dollar and had no more money. "I can remember to this day so vividly like it was yesterday, because that's the day I became a wealthy man. That's the day that scarcity ended in me."

Tony has told this story many times, and each time he inspires more people. The Greek philosopher Aristotle once surmised that the essence of life is "to serve others and do good." We must be of service to others, and that service must come from an altruistic place, not a desire to make ourselves feel good. But there certainly are benefits. If your intentions for volunteering are selfless, and you volunteer regularly, you will live longer, according to a 2012 study in the journal *Health Psychology*.

According to the National Alliance on Mental Illness (NAMI), "A 2020 study conducted in the United Kingdom found those who volunteered reported being more satisfied with their lives and rated their overall health as better. Respondents who volunteered for at least one month also reported having better mental health than those who did not volunteer."[53] In other words, you can live longer, feel better, and have better mental health if you volunteer. You should all be running to sign up right now! And it doesn't have to be volunteering in the strict sense of the definition. You can find other ways to be of service too. In Lewis Howes's book *The School of Greatness*, he highlights his favorite TED talk about the Guerilla Gardener, a guy named Ron Finley. "Guerilla" in this context means using a "hit-and-run" tactic. Ron sneaks into vacant land, plants a garden, and then "runs" away. He performs maintenance on his gardens, though, so he does revisit them— unlike combatants. Ron has been planting vegetable gardens across South Central Los Angeles for years just for fun. Howes says that "he simply does this as a random act of kindness to give back and make his community that much more colorful and fruitful. He takes pride in his community and adds his gifts to it."

The School of Greatness was one of the first personal development books I read. I took so much out of it. "Without service, achievement is empty," Howes writes in chapter 8, "Live a Life of Service." That resonated with what I was doing with public outreach during my time at NASA. I just wanted to teach others about space, share the excitement, and help them out. Every time I could fulfill a request for a NASA speaker, I did. I wanted to use my skills to the best of my ability to help out in my own unique way. Eventually this work became my self-employment because I realized that I could be of service to more people if I had full control over how I did what I was doing and did not have to fight through NASA red tape. That's one of the main reasons I am a former NASA Rocket Scientist. I wanted to serve others on the front lines and not in a cubical designing spaceships anymore.

DARE 8.1

Where can you be of service to others in your life? What random acts of kindness can you start doing? What organizations or events can you start to volunteer at?

Being of service is something you do without the expectation of reciprocation. Expectation means you have a strong belief that something will happen in exchange for what you give. True service is essentially to give freely, without expectation of return. Otherwise, we anticipate getting something and plan for it, which may give us hope or excitement. We create a fantasy in our head of what it is going to be like, how we will feel, and what we will experience. This anticipatory emotion actually signals the release of dopamine, the "feel-good" hormone.

But when things do not turn out as we wanted, we can be disappointed, and that can cause a cascade of negativity. Professor Wolfram Schultz at Cambridge University in England has done some of the best research on the brain regarding expectations.[54, 55] He studies the link between dopamine and reward activities. Schultz found that when we receive a surprise reward, like a bonus at work, our brain releases more dopamine than if we got something expected, like a raise. Nevertheless, expectation causes us to start to feel good before anything ever happens. Our thoughts get us into a state of belief, which then triggers our brain to start releasing dopamine. It's the pleasure of the journey on the way to the destination. Like the thesis to Paulo Coelho's *The Alchemist*, the reward is the journey itself, rather than the destination.

When we hold an unmet expectation—when the fantasy does not become reality—the story of dopamine gets tragic. When we expect a reward and don't get it—a raise, a thank-you for doing something, or someone else being of service back to you—our dopamine levels fall steeply. This leaves you in pain, frustration, and potentially anger. This also leads to a minor threatening response. Your brain is now positioning itself to be protective, defensive against a perceived threat: reward was expected, reward was not received, something must be off or wrong, so we must be prepared for danger. When dopamine levels are too low, the number of connections per second in the brain falls. Not good. This makes it harder for us to focus and be open, curious, or interested.

DARE 8.2

Can you think of a time when you set expectations and they were not met? How did you feel? What did you do? Are there current expectations you're holding when doing something or holding for someone that cause your dopamine levels to fall? How can you alter your expectations in these situations to stabilize your dopamine?

So be of service in a genuine way. Help others, whether in random acts of kindness or in a structured volunteering organization. Have no expectation of getting anything in return. That is not what this practice is about. Just because you act a certain way or are willing to do something doesn't mean anyone else will. We see this time and time again, especially in romantic relationships where one partner does something in hopes of reciprocation and gets upset when it doesn't happen: "But I did all these things for you! Why don't you do them for me?" We cannot expect others to do for us the things we do for others. Should that deter us from doing them? Absolutely not. Give your love genuinely, without expectation of reward in return.

We need to consciously alter what we expect. In the realm of being of service, we need to do it altruistically. In the other realms of our life, we have the ability to set our own expectations. That's easy to say, yet insanely difficult to implement. By default we set expectations based on our own experiences, maybe from how we were raised as children or from prior situations in life. Modifying these default expectations may be the highest mountain you need to climb, the farthest galaxy you need to travel to. And time and time again you'll have to make the journey. By implementing all of *The Practices* you will make the journey to your distant galaxy less grueling. As with all the obstacles we're overcoming, all the design challenges we need to work through, success requires a consistent, long-term effort. Again, we're talking about lifestyle changes here, not a magic six-week course that changes your entire state of mind and then you're good. Nope. The practice, this lifestyle, is rent that's due each day, and you need to make conscious efforts by creating habits to live the Phoenix Mentality.

CHAPTER NINETEEN

Practice 9:
Never Stop Learning

Always stay a student.
—FRANK SHAMROCK

ON AUGUST 29, 1997, in Scotts Valley, California, Reed Hastings founded Netflix.[56] At this time Blockbuster video was the undisputed champion of video rentals. Hastings said he actually created the company because he did not want to pay the $40 fine Blockbuster charged him. At its peak, Blockbuster had about nine thousand stores across the United States. Guess how many are left today. One. A single store still exists in Bend, Oregon, as of September 2022. Netflix has a current revenue of nearly $30 billion. What happened? Why did Netflix overtake Blockbuster in the video-rental arena and become the behemoth it is today?

Because Blockbuster got cocky. The team there stopped learning.

At NASA, Systems Engineers integrate the spacecraft and are responsible for the entire vehicle coming together like a puzzle and working flawlessly. We say the best Systems Engineers have knowledge like a T. They have mastery, or in-depth knowledge, in one specific area—for example, mechanical engineering. That's the vertical line of the T. The horizontal line represents the remaining disciplines. The expert mechanical engineer also has good knowledge in electrical, thermal, propulsion, telecommunication, software, command and data handling, attitude control, instruments, and ground systems. Switch out the vertical line of mechanical engineering for any of the previously listed disciplines.

The best Systems Engineers start with knowledge shaped like a T, but to continue on, to evolve, to be the best of the best, they must increase their knowledge and add more vertical lines. That is, they must approach mastery in another discipline, and then another, then another, until their T looks like a wall of 2x4s in a house frame. Depth of mastery in numerous areas creates the overall best mastery. Even Rocket Scientists need to continue to become better Rocket Scientists over and over again.

Too bad Blockbuster didn't understand this. Blockbuster didn't adapt with evolving technology and society. They were comfortable in their ways, how they did things, and didn't want to change. Netflix was agile and innovated. We might even say that Netflix's middle name is Innovation. Blockbuster was reluctant to come to terms with a new way of doing business. They did for a while forgo the late fees and even started up an online DVD rental system (Netflix's original business). But at heart Blockbuster was basically stubborn and wanted to remain rooted in a comfortable way of operating. It failed to be a student of the world and to continue learning, which ultimately led to its demise.

Change is inevitable and we must evolve with it, or we'll be left behind, especially with regard to technology. There is always a new gadget or app coming out that can do things better, faster, cheaper—or maybe do things that have never been done before. New generations always think they know more than previous generations, and up to a point they do. Children will eventually become more knowledgeable than their parents. That's how the world works. We're not talking intellect or smarts specifically, but in the general sense of what is. At some point, the child will exceed the parent in utilization of technology and awareness of what's possible. Video communication to anyone around the world is common sense to Gen Z. The Silent Generation and some Baby Boomers have a hard time fathoming this and figuring out how to use it.

Moore's Law delivers exponential improvements in all aspects of the world connected to digital life, which is more and more of it. We're learning and growing faster than ever before. We must put in the work to keep learning. This practice is about active learning. Passive acquisition of knowledge will not boost you in your journey. As much as we may wish we can sleep on a book as a pillow and absorb its knowledge, or just be present in a lecture to acquire the information, that's not reality. Make the time to put in the effort and actively acquire new information to expand your horizons and give you breadth in the ever-increasing data of the world.

I believe that you are never done learning. "With accomplishment comes a growing pressure to pretend that we know more than we do. To pretend we already know everything. *Scientia infla* (knowledge puffs up)," wrote Ryan Holiday in *Ego Is the Enemy*. Stay a forever student. Remain aware that there is more, and don't be overconfident in yourself. Success can tempt us to think we're done, that we've accomplished the goal. But that is not the case. "Mastery," writes Holiday, "is a fluid, continual process."

No matter what your academic, career, personal, or age status, you will always continue to learn. Not just in the sense of classwork and work experience, but also learning about life from other people. I place no restrictions on who you can learn from. Even if you hold a PhD, you can learn from the high school dropout, the hobo living in the alley, the teenager working at McDonald's as their first job. Each of these individuals sees life in a different way. Their perspective is different from yours, and you can take aspects from them to improve your own life.

You see the hobo living in the alley. He wakes up every morning and goes to bed every night knowing that he will get wet if it rains. Yet he continues to live his life, and you can even catch a smile on his face from time to time. He is able to find joy and happiness even in his situation. You can take away his aspect of appreciating the little things and finding joy in the darkest of places.

Yes, it is extremely beneficial to surround yourself with amazing people, and you definitely should do so! However, don't forget to notice and appreciate the rest of the people in this world continuing to live day-to-day without the things you take for granted and complain about.

Let us learn not only from those "better" than us (I use "better" in a sense here of personal accomplishment in the business and academic world) but also from those who we perceive to be not as successful. A combination of both will open you up to a world you may never have seen before. Combine them into your own remarkable perspective to achieve even greater accomplishments for yourself, get you out of a rut, or just get yourself started in achieving happiness and success in life.

One of the physicists who helped develop the hydrogen bomb, John Wheeler, once said, "As our island of knowledge grows, so does the shore of our ignorance." The more we learn and know, the more we're aware that there is so much more that we do not know. Another way to think about it is that the bucket of knowledge is ever expanding. Every time you add knowledge to your bucket, the bucket grows in size. You will never fill up your bucket, so you should always be learning.

DARE 9.1

What's something you've always wanted to learn but just haven't got around to yet? Maybe it's another language. Maybe it's a technical skill like photo editing or welding. Maybe it's how the solar cycles of the sun are potentially affecting El Niño and La Niña. Get started on expanding your brain.

In our forever process of learning, we cast ego aside and lean into humility, knowing how much we do not know. In Buddhism, humility is being deeply connected with the practice of the Four Abodes: loving-kindness, compassion, empathetic joy, and equanimity.[57] We must learn to detach from ourselves, to ease our suffering along this journey. We shall not criticize others and praise oneself, but praise others and look deep within the self to see where we can improve. Remaining open to learning, open to growth, is mission-critical for your voyage. The Phoenix Mentality embraces continuous learning and avoiding an inflated sense of self. When we're open to learning forever, we are students of the world, allowing us to be agile.

As you know, course corrections are essential along our way. Being agile allows us to make them fluidly without too much effort. Think of your voyage like traversing a slackline. Quick, violent movements create a chaotic response in the slackline and your body. The key to a successful slackline traverse is to be slow, steady, and have soft, subtle corrective movements. Success requires a constant balance of moving forward, being aware of your surroundings, responding to changes in movement, and being patient.

DARE 9.2

In what area of your life do you need to rein in the ego a bit? Where can you embody more humility?

I'm no brain surgeon (I'm just a Rocket Scientist!), but I can imagine the brain surgeons out there continue to study, to learn, and to implement new methods and processes to improve surgical performance and success rates. This concept isn't rocket science, nor is it brain surgery. Continue to learn throughout your journey and your life. Don't get left out with the old; be swept in with the new. Any other clichés I can add in here? (I just really wanted to use that rocket science/brain surgery bit....)

When you stop learning, you die, at least metaphorically. We saw it with Blockbuster. On your trajectory and even once you've reached your destination, keep learning. Learn along the way, and learn once you reach the top of the mountain. As you sit on top of the mountain expanding your knowledge, you will see more mountains in the distance. Each time you learn more, you'll recognize there are more mountains out there that you've yet to summit. You are looking at the expanding shore of ignorance. As you venture out and summit another, you'll see even more mountains to summit. The experience never ends. To achieve your dreams, to live the Phoenix Mentality, you must commit to learning in perpetuity. Are you up for the mission?

CHAPTER TWENTY
Let's Get to Work

He who is not courageous enough to take
risks will accomplish nothing in life.
—MUHAMMAD ALI

TOO MANY PEOPLE out there are what I call "personal development junkies" who read book after book, maybe even attending the conferences the authors put on. But they don't take actions to effectively pursue their goals. They get hyped on the excitement of potential, and it stops there. They feel motivation, hope, faith that things will work out, but they are waiting for something to happen. The hard truth is that will never work. There is no magical experience that will occur and change your life around from acquiring knowledge. You must put in the actual work, make changes, take an action. As George Bernard Shaw said, "Don't wait for opportunity, create it."

I began this book by sharing my story of how I used NASA's Concept Maturity Levels and The Practices I have refined in my own life not only to dig myself out of a deep and dangerous emotional crisis, but also to achieve my dreams. You are here because you wanted to learn something new, gain perspective, and get an attitude tune-up. You may have felt stuck or uncertain. I certainly did ten years ago (when I wish I had had this book). But now we have proof that there are no limits, that even up against adversity as large as the entire world, change can be made. We know the Levels that NASA and so many Famous Launchers have used to make their dreams a reality. And we learned what it takes to develop a Phoenix Mentality with The Practices. The Proof, The Process, and The Practices: each is an element that adds up to give you the recipe you need to achieve success.

The story of me becoming a NASA Rocket Scientist; The Disruptors; and the stories of Automobiles, Planes, Rockets, Nuclear Energy, Music, and Moore's Law showed us what limitless possibilities look like. The NASA Design Levels showed that the path to walk is having an idea, believing in it, finding out different ways to approach it, picking an approach, and then taking actionable steps to implement it.

LEVEL 1: COCKTAIL NAPKIN
Your idea, the inspiration, the aha moment,
the dream you want to achieve.

LEVEL 2: INITIAL FEASIBILITY
Belief in yourself. It is possible to achieve
what you want to achieve.

LEVEL 3: TRADE SPACE
What options are there to make your dream a reality?

LEVEL 4: POINT DESIGN
What is plan A? What is the best path
forward to achieve your dream?

LEVEL 5: CONCEPT BASELINE
Take action! Go for it. Apply, pitch, create.

REFINE, ITERATE, NEVER GIVE UP

Now it's time to get to work. Incorporating The Practices will take time. Just as it takes multiple years to design a spacecraft, not capable of performing flawlessly, but capable of enduring through almost any circumstance, integrating The Practices is a process. Slowly but surely each one will become a foundational block, an anchor, a pillar, that roots you through your trajectory with the Phoenix Mentality.

The Practices

Practice 1: Mental Health & Outlets

Practice 2: Health & Fitness

Practice 3: Motivation Along the Way

Practice 4: Creating a Support Network

Practice 5: Relentless Work Ethic

Practice 6: Following Up

Practice 7: Kindness & Sincerity

Practice 8: Service to Others

Practice 9: Never Stop Learning

You're engineering your own life. There will be unknown unknowns that will come up and slap you in the face. The Practices will set you up to best take that slap—be a rock, a Chris Rock, if you will. You'll build emotional, mental, physical, and spiritual margin into your life so that you can operate, or at least survive, through the hardships. You might have to go into Safe Mode like a spacecraft, but that's okay; that just is a safeguard for your dreams. That's how spacecrafts survive in space, and how they get there in the first place is with the NASA Design Levels.

THE SINE OF LIFE

To bring everything I have taught you together, I want to introduce you to a concept I call the **Sine of Life**.

In life we have good moments and bad moments, good times and bad times. We could plot them on a graph. Positive experiences and dopamine hits show as +1, negative experiences and lows show as -1. The frequency of the sine plot, a mathematical function, is how often the oscillation between 1 and -1 happens. Uppers with downers occurring all too frequently leave us feeling like life is out of balance. If you plotted your life, how often would you switch from a peak to a valley?

Our goal here is to reduce that frequency. We cannot eliminate the lows altogether, as nice as that may sound. We need the lows to appreciate the highs, and anyway, life isn't fair, so the lows are par for the course.

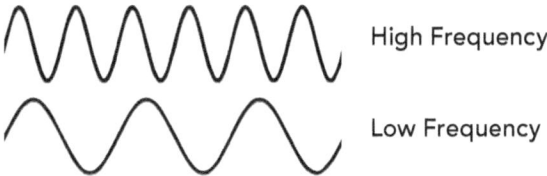

High Frequency

Low Frequency

That's the basic Sine of Life. Now, take it to the next level. If lows are going to be part of your life, what can you do about them? Take a cue from Matthew McConaughey, who wrote this in his book *Greenlights*:

> *The problems we face today eventually turn into blessings in the rearview mirror of life. In time, yesterday's red light leads us to a greenlight. All destruction eventually leads to construction, all death eventually leads to birth, all pain*

eventually leads to pleasure. In this life or the next, what goes down will come up. It's a matter of how we see the challenge in front of us and how we engage with it. Persist, pivot, or concede. It's up to us, our choice every time.

This insight is how you take yourself to the next level: **The Sine + of Life**.

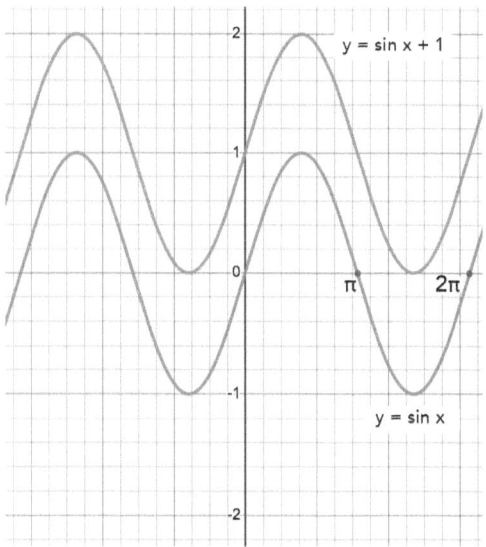

Using The Practices, you can shift your sine curve upward so that instead of centering around zero and moving from 1 to -1, we center around 1 and move from 2 to 0. This means that our highs are higher and our lows are not as low. If we are able to employ all of The Practices effectively, then we realize that there actually is not negative in life. We essentially fortify ourselves from dipping into the negative and only go from positive to neutral. We have our learning moments and our wins, our zeros and our twos respectively. We take everything as it comes, knowing that some are not great, but we do not get bogged down in hatred, anxiety, resentment, frustration. We see a zero as only an obstacle, not a derailment.

Viktor Frankl taught us that we always have a choice, no matter the situation. There is that moment between stimulus and response when we choose. We are the product of our decisions, not our circumstances. If you know how to look at them the right way, negative things that happen in our lives are just red lights that eventually turn green.

My intent with this book is to give you the confidence, motivation, and actionable steps to progress toward your dream. I literally want you to take an action. I want you to do a Level 5. Every single one of us has the ability **To Dare Mighty Things**. Now, Go Take Action!

Action is the foundational key to success. –Pablo Picasso

LOOKING FOR MORE?

Head over to *www.ToDareMightyThings.com*

You don't have to take this voyage alone! We can do it together, literally. We'll go through each level and Practice in a ten week 100% digital online bootcamp. Use the code **TDMTbook10** to get 10% off an online course.

Want to really Dare something Mighty? Signup for personalized coaching where we'll really dive into you—explore who you are and do course corrections as necessary to make sure you're on the right trajectory to becoming your best self in every aspect of life.

Be sure to check us out on social media too and tag us as you go through the Levels and incorporate the Practices into your life!

Instagram: *@ToDareMightyThings*

Twitter: *@DareMghtyThngs*

ACKNOWLEDGMENTS

I would like to thank…

My mom and dad, Nancy and Mike Wydeven, for being the most amazing parents.

My family, blood and forged, you know who you are, for always loving and supporting me through all avenues of my life.

Tom Youmans, Wes Sylvestri, Montez Blair, and Maynard Okereke, who don't truly know how much they helped me survive 2021.

Cory Camp for allowing me to raid your bookshelf to figure out my trim and for being a good friend throughout my dark ages.

Angela Gargano for introducing me to Hal and being supportive through my writing with check-ins and brainstorms.

Dr. Tracy Fanara for being supportive in this process and having conversations that sparked several ideas and concepts that were included in this book.

CJ Finley for providing motivation and content to include in this book, as well as one of the diamond-strong friendships.

Dr. Jacklyn Green, who hired me at NASA JPL and who has been a mentor ever since, even after my leaving.

Prof. Dimitri Mavris, who gave me my graduate research assistantship at Georgia Tech.

Alfred Nash, Randii Wessen, Mark Adler, and Tony Freeman for teaching me the CML process and providing resources during the writing of this book.

David Levine, Dan Goods, and David Rager from the NASA JPL Design Studio for their communication during the writing of this book.

My editor, Hal Clifford, for his insight and work to make *To Dare Mighty Things* a proud accomplishment.

Dr. Lori Bradner for inviting me to give a TEDx talk at Randall Middle School called "Launch Yourself," which was a starting point for the actual writing of this book.

Easy Tiger in Austin, Texas for providing the continuous stream of caffeine and cookies to write and edit this book.

SILVERVOICE, Sandra Esmeralda Rivera for assistance and voice coaching, and ZieM for recording the audiobook version of this text.

All those who laughed at me, whether to my face or behind my back: it gave me some fuel, but I did ultimately do all of it for myself.

Resources: Success Support Tools

Success is no accident. It is hard work,
perseverance, learning, studying, sacrifice and
most of all, love of what you are doing.
—PELE

THIS SECTION IS jam packed with an assortment of tools that I've found to be effective over my years and from connecting with others on their own journeys. Plenty of these notions have been used and promoted by some of the biggest names out there. However, I am not saying do all of these, especially at the same time. I fell into that trap myself in 2021. I was doing it all but wasn't feeling any different; I was actually sliding backward, being more hard on myself. Every single day I would work out; five days of the week I'd be doing two-a-days. I did ice baths. I journaled. I did two ten-minute meditations a day. I did two gratitude lists, one upon waking and one right before bed. Tapped into my Happiness Arsenal almost every day. I had an extremely strict morning and night routine. I was reading books. All of this, Every Single Day. And my therapist pointed out that I was trying to be "perfect," which is unattainable, and that I was using all modalities instead of focusing on the ones most appropriate for my current situation. I cut back, I improved, I gained clarity, and I gave myself grace.

We've talked about some of these already, and this is most definitely not an extensive list. There are more things I find to be beneficial as I continue on my journey. Put these tools in your shed, and take them out as you need/want to use them. Like actual tools—I've had a literal toolbox in the garage and I've only used like five of the one hundred tools in it. But they are there if I ever need them. Just like the content in this section. Find the Success Support Tools that work best for you. Give 'em a try.

Some of these are active activities that you reflect on in the moment, some are work done to reflect back on when needed, others are habits or tips. I've done all of these activities multiple times and find something new from each one. I like to redo them often, some every couple of months, some once a year, and others every couple of years. It's great to look at and see the transformation and progress throughout them. Some things remain the same, and others change.

LIFE WHEEL

Life Wheel is a form with a coloring/shading exercise. It gives you insight into the many areas of your life and how you are balancing all of them. Which ones you're leaning into and which ones you are ignoring. Just search "Life Wheel" on the internet, and several activities will come up. All of them are pretty good to choose from. I like to find one I can print off rather than an online questionnaire to fill out. Doing it by hand means you're putting more intentional effort into it. Just like writing in a journal versus typing on a computer. It makes you go slower and concentrate more and really feel it out.

HAPPINESS ARSENAL

We talked about this in Practice 3: Motivation Along the Way. This is a reminder to continually revisit to add things to your Happiness Arsenal. It could even be as small as a random encounter that provided you with joy. A stranger on a walk who complimented your shoes. Keep expanding this useful tool.

WHEN TRIGGERED, READ THIS

"When Triggered, Read This" is a note on my phone, pinned to the top with this as the title. There are moments that will trigger us in our lives, that may bring up past traumas or irk us in some way. Creating a tool to use in those moments can be helpful. You become aware you are triggered and then go read your note. Below is what mine says.

Remember the lessons from:

- *The Peaceful Warrior*
- *Greenlights*
- *Man's Search for Meaning*
- *Codependent No More*
- *The Four Agreements*
- *Ego Is the Enemy*

It may not seem like it right now, but everything is going to be OK. This is temporary. The feelings are real and it sucks, but it will pass because you get to choose your response. You are strong, smart, lovable, and worthy. This is just a yellow or red light that's a green light. Roll through it, be the peaceful warrior. You got this.

WHEN DISTRESSED

This is another note on my phone, also pinned at the top. It's an abridged version of the Happiness Arsenal. These items are easily accessible and can be immediately implemented. Below is what mine says.

- *Social (texts & FaceTimes)*
- *Fitness*
- *Distance (Go get a Smoothie)*
- *Podcasts*
- *Funny Movie/Disney*
- *Comedy (TV/TikTok)*
- *Journal*
- *Caffeine*
- *Breathe*
- *Meditate*

ANXIETY CHECKLIST

Another and the last note pinned on my phone. If you are feeling anxious about a situation that just occurred, use this note in an attempt to relieve some of the anxiety. This one is a combination of questions to ask in general, questions about the situation itself, and a list of calming exercises. Below is what mine says.

Checklist
- *Is everyone safe?*
- *When are you able to talk about it?*
- *What are your concerns?*
- *Be calm.*

Questions
- *Was something a mistake or possibly forgotten?*
- *Is this similar to something before?*
- *Can anything be done about it at this exact moment?*
- *Be calm.*

Calming Exercises
- *Breathing*
- *Headspace App*
- *Journaling*
- *Go for a run.*
- *Distract yourself.*
- *Think of how you are right now compared to what you want to be.*

JOURNALING

Have either a blank journal or one with prompts. I advise setting this out on your desk, table, or someplace you are frequently so it's a reminder when you see it with a pen right on top of it.

GRATITUDE LIST

Start each day and/or end each night with writing down three things that you are grateful for. I've done this on a whiteboard, a blank notebook or journal, and most recently using a prompted five-minute gratitude journal.

BOOK LIST

I keep a list of all the books I've read. I even have a Google Doc that has all the quotes from each book that I highlighted. That way I can go back through just a single document and see what stuck out to me. I also have a list of future books that I would like to read. And I always have two or three books on hand that are in my queue to tackle next.

MORNING & NIGHT ROUTINES

Establishing routines to start and end your day can be quite helpful, and a lot of successful people swear by their routines.

FITNESS GOALS/EVENTS

I like to sign up for an event. That way I've made a commitment and put money on the line. I've already spent the money, so I feel bad if I don't put in the effort and do it. Also it gives me something to work toward, to focus on.

THERAPY

We talked about this in Practice 1: Mental Health & Outlets. Use it. Please. More of us need to utilize this tool.

ACCOUNTABILITY PARTNER

Find someone to check in with. Hold them accountable to what they say and want, and have them hold you to what you're working on. I have a standing meeting every Thursday with one of my best friends for us to FaceTime and check in. We talk about goals, business ideas, progress of projects, romantic relationships, family, and life.

CALENDAR/PLANNER

Keep track of your schedule. Whether that's writing things down in a physical planner or in an online calendar. I use Google Calendar for all of my scheduling. I use different colors for different categories to help keep things organized. And then it sends me reminders too. That's something a physical planner doesn't do that I really need at times. I'll get so busy or deep into a task and forget that I have something to do. Then my phone pings me thirty minutes before.

WRITING THINGS DOWN

Literally write your goals down. A piece of paper, a Post-it note, or on your phone. Write things down. I also write down to-do lists all the time. It helps me stay organized, and it gives me a much higher chance of success that I'll actually get these things done.

VISUAL CUES

This one I really like. Put visual cues in your life. I wrote motivational phrases on Post-it notes and put them on my most frequented places in my grad school apartment. I put them on the bathroom mirror, microwave, fridge, and next to the door handle. I even did this in 2021 with phrases like "You Are Worthy" and "You Deserve Awesome" on my TV and computer.

COMMITMENT DEVICES

These are things like self-punishment or rewards for doing or not doing something. If you run every day this week, you can have pizza and ice cream on Sunday. Or if you don't get these three things done by next Wednesday, you have to do one hundred burpees or donate $500 to charity.

FRONT PAGE OF THE NEWSPAPER

This one is really simple. I make every decision and do every action with the thought "If this was to be on the front page of the newspaper, how would I feel about that?" We might have to change this to "Trending on Twitter" nowadays.

THE STORY I'M TELLING MYSELF IS...

The last one we'll cover here is a communication tool when there is a misunderstanding or disagreement or uncertainty with someone. You literally start by saying, "The story I'm telling myself is..." and then continue to state your thoughts. As an example, "The story I'm telling myself is that you did that on purpose to hurt me and it makes me feel bad." This avoids accusing and is the new way to approach the "I feel" situations we may have been taught as a child.

Now it may seem a little overwhelming to try to tackle it all. So don't. Work up to it. One at a time. And here's the thing, the more of these you start to incorporate into your life and take advantage of, eventually the less and less you'll need to actively use them. They'll become ingrained habits. It'll be second nature to you, and that is amazing. It's a process. This will take a long time to establish, which is why we need to get started right away. This proactive approach will be so beneficial to you when those obstacles show up in your way. Preventive maintenance rather than reactive approaches is the way to be sustainable on your journey.

NASA Design Levels in Detail

LEVEL 1: COCKTAIL NAPKIN

Science: What does the mission intend to accomplish?

Engineering: What system is envisioned?

The science questions have been well articulated, the type of science observations needed for addressing these questions have been proposed, and a rudimentary sketch of the mission concept and high-level objectives have been created. The essence of what makes the idea unique and meaningful has been captured.

Psyche Mission: Grassroots idea from Principal Investigator L.T. Elkins-Tanton. *Is there a compelling* Discovery *mission to visit the interior of a body for the first time, by sending a mission to an iron metal asteroid?*

LEVEL 2: INITIAL FEASIBILITY

Science: Top-level science objectives: Quantify objectives in order to allow validation of physical feasibility.

Engineering: High-level comparison to similar systems: Assess flight system feasibility; identify new developments and key performance parameters.

The idea is expanded and questioned on the basis of feasibility, from a science, technical, and programmatic viewpoint. Lower-level objectives have been specified, key performance parameters have been quantified, and basic calculations have been performed. These calculations, to first-order, determine the viability of the concept.

Psyche Mission: *Is the science worth doing? Will the science objectives be achieved?* An A-Team study was conducted to focus on the science feasibility, resulting in refined science questions, potential architectures, and deemed financially viable within the cost cap by using the Dawn mission as an analogy.

    A. Is Psyche a core, or did it never undergo melting?
    B. What are the relative ages of its surface regions?
    C. Do small metal bodies incorporate the light elements expected to be inside Earth's high-pressure core?
    D. Did Psyche form under more oxidizing or more reducing conditions than Earth's core?
    E. What is the unique topography of this metal world?

LEVEL 3: TRADE SPACE

Science: Prioritized objectives; investigations: Explore multiple architectures for achieving objectives; evaluate science value, mission cost bin, mission risk for each architecture.

Engineering: Accurate architectures: Evaluate system design in response to alternate architectures.

Exploration has been done around the science objectives and architectural trades between the spacecraft system, ground system, and mission design to explore impacts on and understand the relationship between science return, cost, and risk.

Psyche Mission: Various mission design analysis was conducted with different propulsion (chemical & solar electric) and launch vehicle options. Then a second A-Team study was conducted focusing on the payload and instrument options. The results were four potential architectures, the identification of potential instrument partnerships and contributors, and minimum to maximum mission cost ranges.

LEVEL 4: POINT DESIGN

Science: Baseline & threshold; traceability matrix: Document selected design: Traceability matrix (science, to instruments, to data products, to key mission features); baseline and threshold mission attributes

Engineering: System & subsystem block diagrams and configuration & CAD drawings: To establish initial flight system design

A specific design with a cost that returns the desired science has been selected within the Trade Space and defined down to the level of major subsystems with acceptable margins and reserves. Subsystems trades have been performed.

Psyche Mission: After doing architecture-level trades (the feedback loop), a TeamX concurrent engineering study was conducted for the down-selected architecture to get a first-level design of propulsion, avionics, thermal, mechanical, and power subsystems as well as estimate the overall lifecycle mission cost.

LEVEL 5: BASELINE CONCEPT

Science: Concept baseline requirements: Detailed Traceability Matrix with all top-level science requirements (mission drivers) identified

Engineering: Document design: To enable external evaluations and costing

Implementation approach has been defined including partners, contracting mode, integration and test approach, cost and schedule. This maturity level represents the level needed to write a NASA step 1 proposal (for competed projects) or hold a Mission Concept Review (for assigned projects).

Psyche Mission: TeamX played the red team during a mock review process, accessing the science and technical merit of the mission. Then a Psyche Step I proposal was submitted to NASA HQ.

Example Summaries

Real-World Example

1. Kevin watched *October Sky* and wanted to design spaceships for NASA and become a Rocket Scientist.
2. Kevin believed in himself and knew that "if you put your mind to it, you can accomplish anything" (quote from one of his favorite movies, *Back to the Future*).
3. Kevin saw he could get a degree in mechanical engineering and then an advanced degree in aerospace engineering. He could go to Georgia Tech, MIT, Maryland, Arizona.
4. Kevin chose Georgia Tech as the place he wanted to go for graduate school.
5. Kevin applied to Georgia Tech. Got rejected, followed up, got accepted.

NASA Example (Psyche Mission)

1. Is there a compelling *Discovery* mission to visit the interior of a body for the first time, by sending a mission to an iron metal asteroid?
2. An A-Team study was conducted to focus on the science feasibility resulting in refined science questions, potential architectures, and deemed financially viable within the cost cap by using the Dawn mission as an analogy.

3. Various mission design analysis was conducted with different propulsion (chemical & solar electric) and launch vehicle options. Then a second A-Team study was conducted focusing on the payload and instrument options. The results were four potential architectures, the identification of potential instrument partnerships and contributors, and minimum to maximum mission cost ranges.

4. After doing architecture-level trades (the feedback loop), a TeamX concurrent engineering study was conducted for the down-selected architecture to get a first-level design of propulsion, avionics, thermal, mechanical, and power subsystems as well as estimate the overall lifecycle mission cost.

5. TeamX played the red team during a mock review process, accessing the science and technical merit of the mission. Then a Psyche Step I proposal was submitted to NASA HQ.

Sylvester Stallone Example

1. Stallone watched the Muhammad Ali vs. Chuck Wepner fight and was immediately inspired.

2. Stallone is the textbook definition of Level 2, "belief in yourself," because damn...dropping out of college, living in poverty, doing crap jobs to survive to audition, selling your dog...dude had guts and a rock-solid confidence in his abilities as an actor.

3. Stallone then needed to find a way to sell his *Rocky* script, to shop around to several producers and try to get them to buy the screenplay. What are the different ways he could get this script in front of people?

4. Plan A was him as the star role; there was no Plan B.

5. Stallone was so determined to achieve his dreams and believed in himself so strongly that he accepted $25,000 for the script, rather than $350,000, on the premise he would maintain the starring role.

REFERENCES

1   https://voicesofdemocracy.umd.edu/roosevelt-strenuous-life-1899-speech-text/#:~:text=Far%20better%20it%20is%20to,knows%20not%20victory%20nor%20defeat

2   https://www.latimes.com/science/la-xpm-2012-aug-05-la-sci-sn-mars-curiosity-gets-final-message-from-engineers-20120805-story.html

3   https://puzzling.stackexchange.com/questions/5656/when-does-11-3

4   https://www.homemadetools.net/forum/new-york-times-mocked-robert-goddard-inventor-liquid-fueled-rocket-1920-a-57173

5   https://dorksideoftheforce.com/2019/05/29/star-wars-gap-rotj-tpm/

6   https://www.news.com.au/technology/innovation/inventions/the-life-changing-inventions-the-experts-said-were-impossible/news-story/8c8b0e58532b329d1b6f97c3dfee9fcc

7   https://jplteamx.jpl.nasa.gov/

8   https://trs.jpl.nasa.gov/bitstream/handle/2014/44299/13-3547_A1b.pdf?sequence=1

9   https://trs.jpl.nasa.gov/bitstream/handle/2014/44457/13-4156_A1b.pdf?sequence=1

10 https://www.glassdoor.com/Award/Best-Places-to-Work-LST_KQ0,19.htm

11 https://www.eandvgroup.com/the-cocktail-napkin-hall-of-fame/

12 https://anecdotage.com/anecdotes/young-steven-spielberg-be-sure-youre-right-then-go-ahead

13 https://philipchircop.wordpress.com/2014/02/18/believe-in-yourself/

14 https://alltimeshortstories.com/the-man-with-a-lamp/

15 https://www.forbes.com/sites/chrismyers/2018/02/23/how-to-find-your-ikigai-and-transform-your-outlook-on-life-and-business/?sh=bfd62ff2ed44

16 https://www.wright-brothers.org/History_Wing/Wright_Story/Inventing_the_Airplane/Inventing_the_Airplane_Intro.htm

17 https://www.history.com/topics/inventions/wright-brothers

18   https://www.recordonline.com/story/lifestyle/2011/10/24/tell-me-story-conquering-fear/49862096007/

19   https://professionaltales.com/the-success-story-of-a-triumphant-entrepreneur-sam-walton/#:~:text=In%20July%201962%2C%20Sam%20launched,entrepreneur%20got%20wilder%20for%20success

20   https://www.newsweek.com/story-farmer-nasa-astronaut-jose-hernandez-rejected-11-times-1601533

21   https://www.thecalifornian.com/story/news/2016/10/08/farmer-astronaut-jose-hernandezs-inspiring-story/91757092/

22   https://www.sciencedaily.com/releases/2022/10/221010115407.htm

23   https://www.sciencedaily.com/releases/2022/10/221010115407.htm

24   https://greatist.com/happiness/23-scientifically-backed-ways-reduce-stress-right-now#relax

25   https://podcasts.apple.com/us/podcast/huberman-lab/id1545953110?i=1000576901433

26   https://www.sciencedaily.com/releases/2022/10/221010115407.htm

27   https://www.youtube.com/watch?v=4n-R07zlz1g

28   Yang L, Zhao Y, Wang Y, et al. The effects of psychological stress on depression. Curr Neuropharmacol. 2015;13(4):494-504. doi:10.2174/1570159x1304150831150507

29   https://www.verywellmind.com/negative-self-talk-and-how-it-affects-us-4161304

30   https://hubermanlab.com/dr-peter-attia-exercise-nutrition-hormones-for-vitality-and-longevity/

31   https://www.cnbc.com/2018/05/17/10-highly-successful-people-who-wake-up-before-6-a-m.html

32   https://www.glamourmagazine.co.uk/gallery/morning-routines-of-successful-people

33   https://www.ncbi.nlm.nih.gov/pmc/articles/PMC9268228/

34   https://www.cnbc.com/2022/05/14/harvard-nutritionist-and-brain-expert-avoids-these-foods-that-make-you-tired-and-stressed.html

35   https://hubermanlab.com/the-science-and-use-of-cold-exposure-for-health-and-performance/

36   https://hubermanlab.com/tools-to-manage-dopamine-and-improve-motivation-and-drive/

37   https://www.entrepreneur.com/leadership/these-6-types-of-music-are-known-to-dramatically-improve/325492

38   https://www.nme.com/news/music/various-artists-62-1193425#:~:text=
     Michael%20Phelps%20has%20revealed%20that,the%20start%20of%20
     a%20competition.

39   https://www.vanityfair.com/hollywood/2020/04/the-half-of-it-netflix-
     movie-alice-wu

40   https://courses.washington.edu/pbafhall/514/514%20Readings/
     ProspectTheory.pdf

41   https://www.ncbi.nlm.nih.gov/pmc/articles/PMC5951237/

42   https://www.ncbi.nlm.nih.gov/pmc/articles/PMC6539343/

43   https://www.proquest.com/openview/f98470912aa00f2b6a5f14815c2d671c/
     1?pq-origsite=gscholar&cbl=2036059

44   https://abcnews.go.com/Health/Diet/story?id=3413751&page=1#:~:text
     =The%20researchers%20found%20that%20when,risk%20increased%20
     by%2037%20percent

45   https://en.wikipedia.org/wiki/Stanford_marshmallow_experiment

46   https://www.sciencedirect.com/science/article/pii/S0167268119302641?
     via%3Dihub

47   https://www.basketball-reference.com/leaders/orb_career.html

48   https://www.forbes.com/sites/joefolkman/2015/01/08/top-ranked-
     leaders-know-this-secret-ask-for-feedback/?sh=3fa2c58a3195

49   http://psychology.iresearchnet.com/social-psychology/emotions/facial-
     feedback-hypothesis/

50   https://journals.sagepub.com/doi/abs/10.1177/0956797610363775

51   https://psycnet.apa.org/doiLanding?doi=10.1037%2F0022-3514.80.1.112

52   https://bigthink.com/videos/tony-robbins-the-secret-to-living-is-giving/

53   https://www.nami.org/Blogs/NAMI-Blog/February-2022/How-
     Volunteering-Improves-Mental-Health

54   https://journals.physiology.org/doi/full/10.1152/physiologyonline.
     1999.14.6.249

55   https://docs.google.com/document/d/1QcDuOmHvqNk7D1XHFsjPJcS6jDr
     D1nQt25RSXyNSK7E/edit#

56   https://www.businessinsider.com/rise-and-fall-of-blockbuster#but-trouble-
     was-on-the-horizon-in-1997-as-blockbusters-future-competitor-netflix-
     was-founded-7

57   https://en.wikipedia.org/wiki/Humility#Buddhism

ABOUT THE AUTHOR

Kevin J DeBruin is an expert in NASA's mission & spacecraft design process. He has achieved every goal he's ever set and shares his space & success knowledge to educate and inspire others. Kevin crafts engaging stories to share his expertise with the world in an easy to understand and relatable way. From the best place to find alien life in our solar system to overcoming obstacles to achieve your dreams, he motivates all those he interacts with.

DeBruin's accolades include being a NASA Rocket Scientist, a Masters of Science in Aerospace Engineering from Georgia Tech, designing more than 30 advanced space missions and spacecrafts, author of *To NASA & Beyond* & *The Quick Guide to Adulting*, a two-time TEDx speaker, founder of Space Class, well-respected & trusted space expert & personality, educator, space & science camp instructor, expert space consultant for media companies, spacecraft design course instructor, contract engineer for the aerospace industry, an Eagle Scout, certified personal trainer, American Ninja Warrior, bodybuilder, and 1st place finisher in obstacle course races.

DeBruin specializes in robotic solar system exploration with an expertise in Jupiter's moon Europa. He is a Space Expert with a focus in spacecraft flight system design and utilization of model-based systems engineering. After NASA he worked for a short while at The Aerospace Corporation as a Senior Systems Engineer where he launched two 1.5U CubeSats into Earth orbit.

Learn more about Kevin at *www.kevinjdebruin.com* and on Instragram @kevinjdebruin